CLOTHING STRUCTURE & DESIGN

FIONA PAULSON T

The book is dedicated to all the Fresh minds who like to gain interest and more knowledge over Fabric structures and to also learn the methods of weaving using the techniques. To those who also show interest over the Fashion Industry to create new innovations learning the basics of fabrics.

Contents

Foreword

Persual of Fashion as passion, we would like to give information about basic fabric structure to students who muct gain attention and know the importance of fabric weaving in the fashion field. The clothing structure and deign comes with a mission to open, inform and connect young designers with Industrial knowledge by helping them create innovative fabrics with global attenton, with which they can make the fashion industry more fruitfull to the nation.

Preface

The idea to expose young minds with fabric weaving ideas which evolve them towards the art of weaving fibres into fabrcs has always been our idea.

Clothing Structure and Design is one such book that makes machines, weaving, manufacturing and learning new innovation as its primary aim. The book primarilly makes young minds more about the technical side of innovation and how it helps in the creation of making fabric around the world. This book is a stratergic and student oriented book to develop the innovative skills and creating oneself stronger.

Acknowledgements

This work is complete and successfulonly because of the encouragement and contribution of many good hearted people. We would like to express our sincere gratitude to all those who became the chanel of grace.

We would like to thank our College PSG college of Arts and Science, Coimbatore., Our department Costume design and Fashion and also our Co-staffs for providing the facilities to gain knowledge and allowing us gain more information about our field also our topic.

We thank our friends for their co-ordination to make the book a success, we thank our parents and family for their support. We also cannot finish without thanking the almighty who spread over everywhere.

Prologue

Congratulations!! You are reading this means, you have taken a step closer towards Fashion Industry for developing the idea to design through learning the basics of weaving and also through structure design. Let the book give more knowledge about Clothing Structure and Design.

CHAPTER I

Elements of Woven Design

AIMS & OBJECTIVES

In this chapter we discuss the elements of Elements of woven design & Methods of fabric representation. The main aim of this chapter is to study the draft and lifting plan, construction of elementary weaves – plain, wrap rib, weft rib, twill, modification of twills, satin and sateen weaves – their derivatives

ELEMENTS OF WOVEN DESIGN

Definition

- Woven fabrics are composed of longitudinal warp threads and transverse weft threads interlaced with one another according to the class of structure and form of design that is desired.
- Warp threads are individually known as **ends**
- Weft threads are individually known as **picks** or **filling**

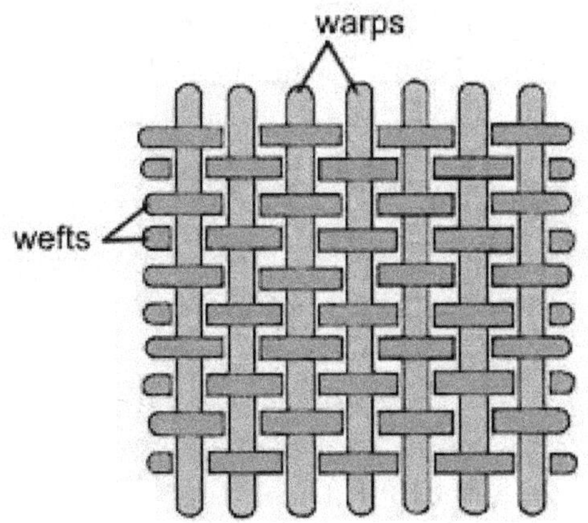

Warp and Weft

CLASSIFICATION OF WOVEN FABRICS

Simple structures

- Ends and picks intersect at right angles to one another and are parallel
- One series of ends and one series of picks are used in the weave

Compound Structures

- It constitutes more than one series of ends or picks.
- Some yarns are ground yarns forming body and some are employed for ornamental purposes like figuring or face yarns.
- Threads may not be parallel in either plane
- Some threads may project out at right angles from fabric surface forming pile

BASIC OPERATIONS IN WOVEN CLOTH PRODUCTION

A loom is a device that causes interlacement two sets of threads, namely, warp and weft threads, to form a fabric. The very first loom in history is the pit loom. Subsequently the handloom was developed and then the power loom. After the advent of power looms, a number of developments have taken place. The very first power looms that had been developed were of the non automatic type. These looms had neither a positive let off device nor a warp stop mechanism or a weft changing mechanism. This demanded a great deal of attention from the weaver. The semi automatic loom was then developed which incorporated two out of the above three mentioned mechanisms. Then the automatic loom was developed which had all the three essential mechanisms, namely, positive let off device, warp stop mechanism and weft replenishment mechanism. The last century saw the development of shuttle less weaving mechanisms.

The hand loom was operated by the weaver using his hands to propel the shuttle from one end to another. The weaver used his foot to operate the healds. The production in this type of loom was obviously very less and thus varied from weaver to weaver. The power loom was operated by power. This reduced the strain of the weaver. Considerable automation has taken place which resulted in lesser strain of the operatives and increasing the production and efficiency of the loom. The shuttle less looms are good examples.

The tappet, dobby and jacquard are warp patterning mechanisms. Among the shuttle looms, the tappet loom is the simplest. It is suitable for weaving up to 8 heald shafts. The dobby loom is suitable for figuring upto 40 heald shafts and the jacquard is suitable for elaborate designs running to several picks. The advantage of the jacquard mechanism is that it can control individual warp ends and hence has a large figuring capacity.

The multiple box mechanism is suitable for weft patterning, particularly in creating checked effects in the fabric. The colouring capacity of the multiple boxes ranges from 2 to 24. The shuttle less looms have the advantage of higher speed and efficiency than the conventional shuttle looms. Also larger weft packages minimize the frequency of weft changes thus improving the loom efficiency.

Schematic Diagram of a loom

- The fabric is produced on the loom. Refer diagram

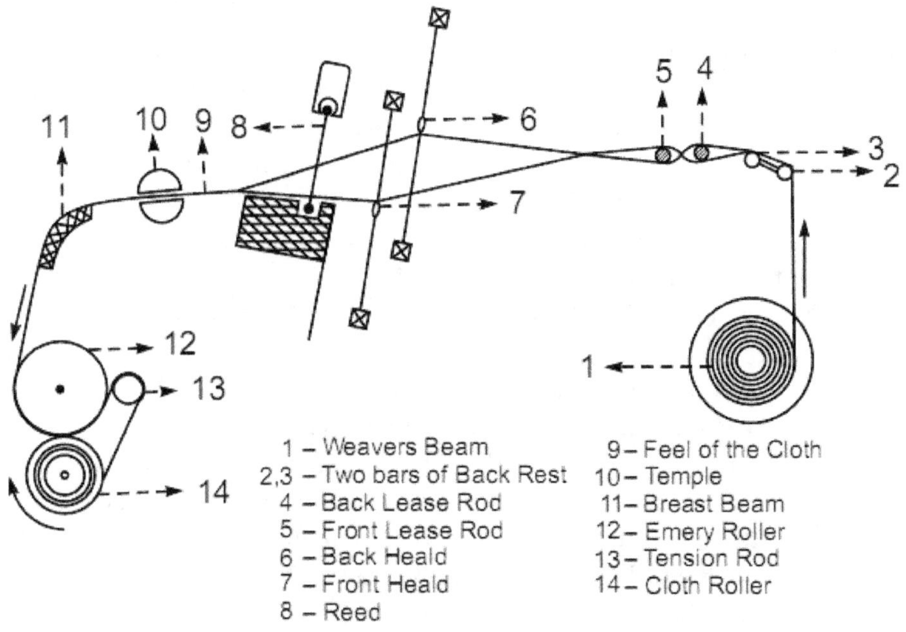

Loom

HEALD SHAFT

This part is related to the shedding mechanism. The heald shaft is made of wood or metal such as aluminum. It carries a number of heald wires through which the ends of the warp sheet pass. The heald shafts are also known as 'heald frames' or 'heald staves'. The number of heald shafts depends on the warp repeat of the weave. It is decided by the drafting plan of a weave. **The main function of the heald shaft is as follows:**

- It helps in shed formation
- It is useful in identifying broken warp threads
- It maintains the order or sequence of the warp threads
- It determines the order of lifting or lowering the required number of healds for a pick. In other words it helps in forming the design or pattern in a fabric.
- It determines the warp thread density in a fabric, i.e. the numbers of heald wires per inch determine the warp thread density per inch.

SLEY OR LAY

It is made of wood and consists of the sley race or race board, reed cap and metal swords carried at either ends. The sley mechanism swings to and fro. It is responsible for pushing the last pick of weft to the fell of the cloth by means of the beat up motion. The sley moves faster when moving towards the fell of the cloth and moves slower when moving backwards. This unequal movement is known as 'eccentricity of the sley'. It is needed in order to perform the beat up and also to give sufficient time for passage of shuttle to pass through the warp shed. The beat up of the lastly laid pick of weft is accomplished through a metal reed attached to the sley.

SHUTTLE

It is basically a weft carrier and helps in interlacement of the weft with the warp threads to form cloth. The shuttle which is made of wood passes from one end of the loom to the other. It travels along the wooden sley race and passes between the top and bottom layers of the warp sheet. The shuttle enters a shuttle box fitted at either ends of the loom, after passing through the warp shed. A shuttle normally weighs about 0.45 kgs.

SHUTTLE BOX

It is the housing for the shuttle and is made of wood. It has a spindle and a picker. It may also accommodate the picker without spindle. The top and side of the box towards the sley race are open. The shuttle dwells inside the box for the intermediate period between two successive picks.

PICKER

The picker is a piece made either of leather or synthetic material. It may be placed on a spindle or grooves in the shuttle box. It is used to drive the shuttle from one box to another. It also sustains the force of the shuttle while entering the box.

REED

It is a metallic comb that is fixed to the sley with a reed cap. The reed is made of a number of wires and the gap between wires is known as dents. Each dent can accommodate one, two or more warp ends. The count of the reed is decided by the number of dents in two inches. The reed performs a number of functions which are enumerated as follows:

(*i*) It pushes the lastly laid pick of weft to the cloth fell

(*ii*) It helps to maintain the position of the warp threads

(*iii*) It acts as a guide to the shuttle which passes from one end of the loom to the other.

(*iv*) It determines the fineness of the cloth in conjunction with the healds.

(*v*) It determines the openness or closeness of the fabric.

There are various types of reed such as ordinary reed, gauze reed, expanding reed, V reed etc.

WARP BEAM

This is also known as the weaver's beam. It is fixed at the back of the loom. The warp sheet is wound on to this beam. The length of warp in the beam may be more than a thousand meters.

BACK BEAM

This is also known as the back rest. It is placed above the weaver's beam. It may be of the fixed or floating type. In the first case the back rest merely acts as a guide to the warp sheet coming from the weaver's beam. In the second case it acts both as a guide and as a sensor for sensing the warp tension.

BREAST BEAM

It is also known as the front rest. It is placed above the cloth roller at the front of the loom and acts as a guide for the cloth being wound on to the cloth roller. The front rest together with the back rest helps to keep the warp yarn and cloth in horizontal position and also maintain proper tension to facilitate weaving.

CLOTH BEAM

It is also known as the cloth roller. The woven cloth is wound on to this roller. This roller is placed below the front rest.

PREPARATORY STEPS FOR WEAVING

Preparing the Weaver's Beam

- Preparatory operations in making up the beam are winding, warping and sizing of the warp yarns
- Sheet of warp yarn consisting of required number of ends are wound into considerable length on a weaver's beam

Specifications for making a beam are :
Type of yarn

a. Number of ends
b. Length of warp
c. Pattern if a cloth with colored stripes is to be produced

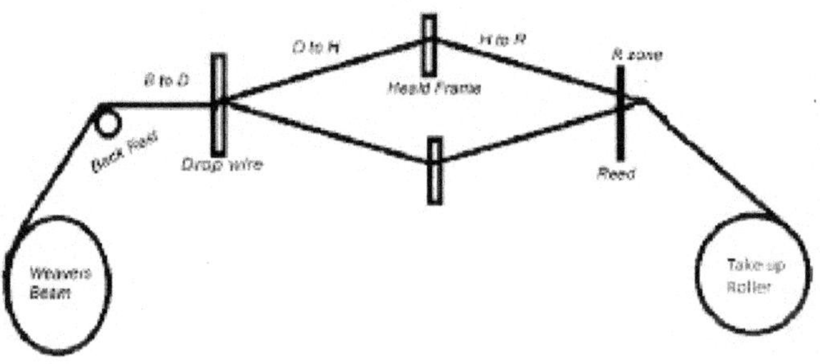

Schematic Structure of the Loom

Preparing the loom

- **Back beam** is also known as the back rest. It is placed above the weaver's beam. It may be of the fixed or floating type. In the first case the back rest merely acts as a guide to the warp sheet coming from the weaver's beam. In the second case it acts both as a guide and as a sensor for sensing the warp tension.
- Warp yarns from the weaver's beam are drawn through the drop wires and then through the healds.

- From the healds they are threaded through the splits of the reed
- Warp interlaces the weft which is supplied by the shuttle through the shed
- Cloth is formed at the fell

- The cloth passes over the breast beam round the take up roller and wound on the cloth roller
- **Drawing-in** is the entering of yarns from a new warp into the weaving elements of a weaving machine namely drop wires, heddles and reed, starting up a new fabric style.
- After the depletion of a warp beam on the weaving machine, if there will be no change in design **tying-in** process is done

WEAVING PROCESS

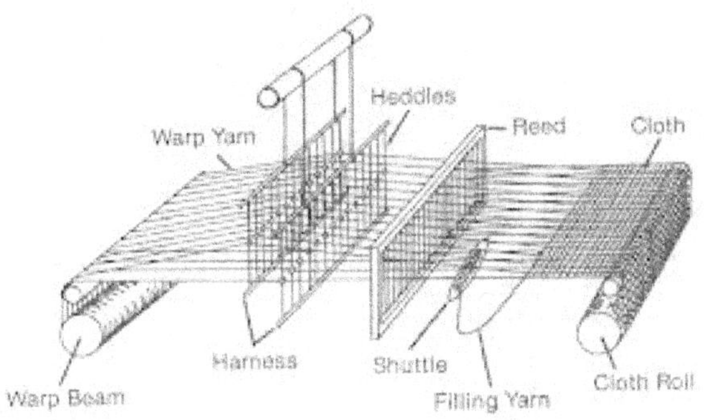

Weaving Loom

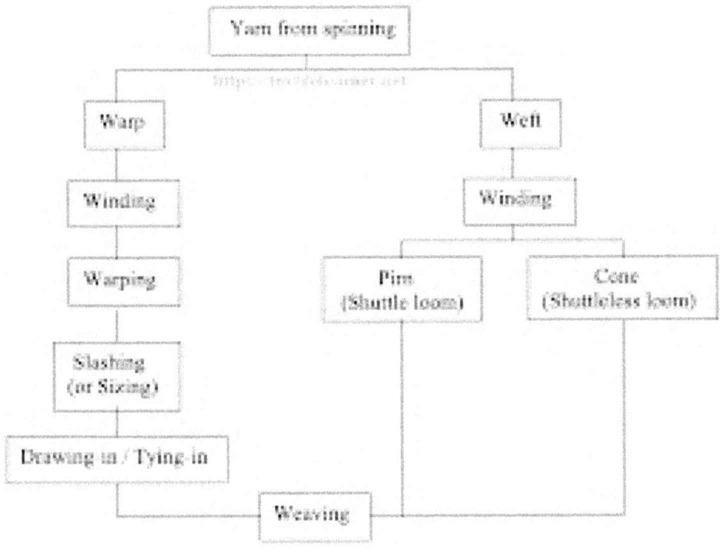

Weaving Process

Primary Motions

Shedding: Separation of warp threads into upper and lower layers forming a shed through which the weft is passed. It is the heart of weaving as it determines the nature of interlacing or the weave.

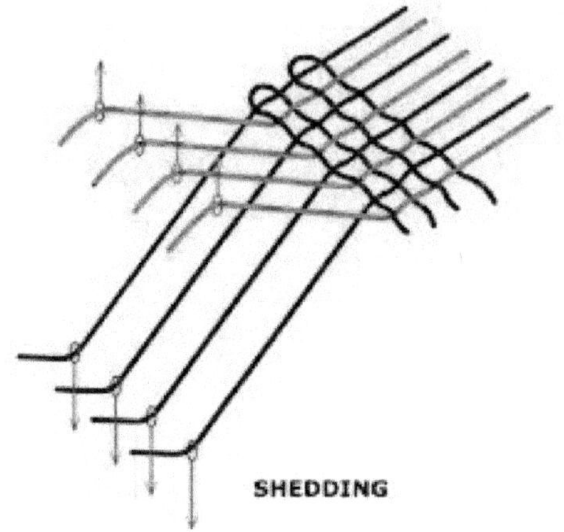

Weaving- Shedding Process

- During this process warp threads are manipulated to produce a given interlacing.
- It is achieved by threading each end through an eye of a heald wire in harness and raising or lowering this wire dependent on whether it is required to lift the end above the weft, or to keep it below the weft during picking.
- In tappet and dobby shedding, heald wires are attached to heald frames or harnesses in which a group of yarns with same interlacement are passed.

In Jacquard shedding individual warp yarns are controlled

i. **Picking:** Insertion of the weft through the shed

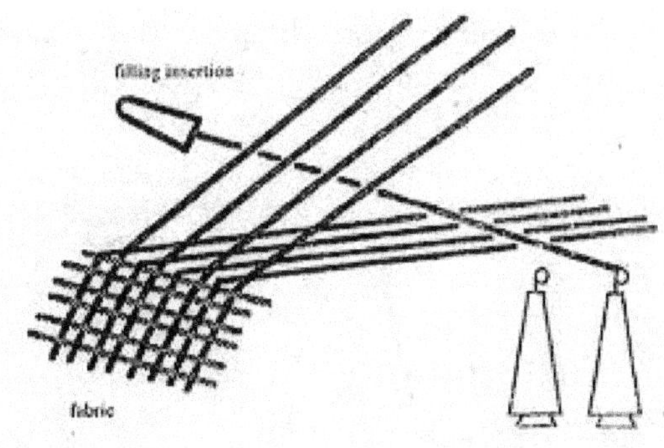

Picking

ii. Beating-up: Pushing the newly inserted weft into the already woven fabric to the point called the fabric fell

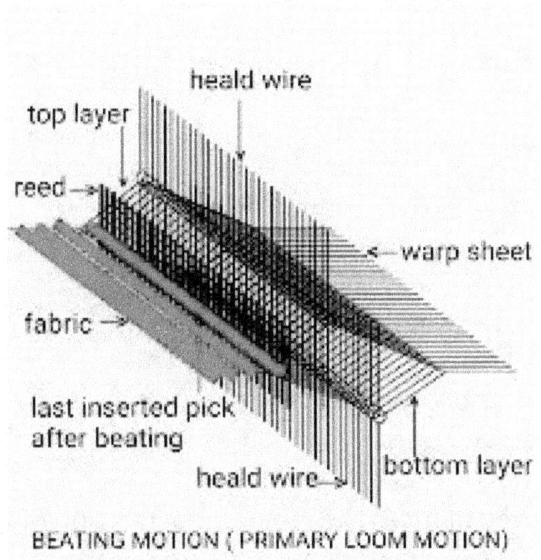

Beating Process

Ancillary motions

i. **Warp pay off/Warp letting-off:** Delivering the warp to the formation zone by unwinding it from the weaver's beam. Determines the rate at which warp is fed forward and tension of the warp yarn

ii. **Cloth take up:** Moving fabric from the formation zone and winding the fabric onto a cloth roller. Determines the speed of cloth withdrawal and the density of spacing of weft picks in the cloth

iii. **The weft color selector:** For weaving crossover or transverse stripes consisting of different kinds or colors of weft. Upto eight different weft threads can be introduced in modern machines.

METHODS OF FABRIC REPRESENTATION
Plan Diagram or interlacing diagram.

Interlacing

- This method is rarely used in designing woven fabrics as they are too laborious to prepare especially for large designs.

- The unit of woven fabric is the point of intersection of a warp end and a weft pick.
- A number of these interlacings combined together in both directions produce a unit of design, or one repeat of the weave.

- The simplest weave, plain weave, requires two ends and two picks as a repeat of design. Successive neighbouring units will be identical with the first.

- This shows that for 1st pick every odd end in the warp will be lowered and every even one will be raised

Canvas Method using design paper also called point paper or squared paper.

- The standard textile design paper is ruled 8 X 8 these being separated by thicker bar lines.
- Point paper is the specific plan of the order of the interlacing of threads.
- Marks are used to denote interlacing of warp over weft and blanks to denote the interlacing warp under weft. Reversal of convention if taken should be indicated.
- In each full repeat of weave every vertical space and every horizontal space must have at least one mark and at least one blank
- Point paper does not indicate configuration of threads in the cloth so it may be supplemented by section diagrams.
- Cross Section Diagram
- Longitudinal Section Diagram

Weave Repeat Unit

- Any weave repeats on a definite number of ends and picks.
- Here is a plain weave. From the diagram, we can see, the 3rd warp thread has the same movement with the 1st, and the 4th warp thread has the same movement with the 2nd. Similarly, the 3rd weft thread is same with the 1st weft thread; the 4th is same with the 2nd

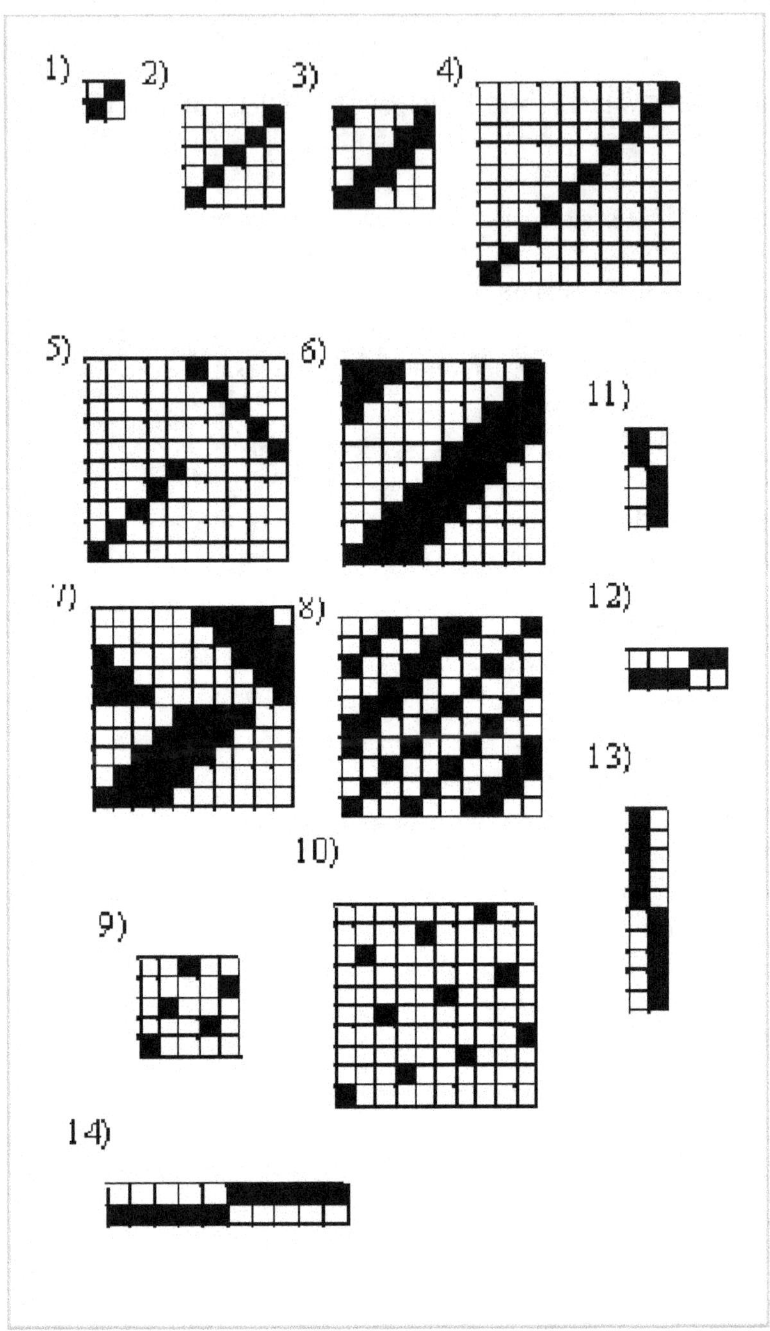

Plain weave- Repeat

- Commencing a weave at a different position will not affect the appearance of the cloth
- Marks and blanks should join correctly at sides, top and bottom of a design to get a continuous and unbroken weave
- **Warp Repeat**: The minimal number of warp threads after which the movements of warp threads repeat.
- **Weft Repeat**: The minimal number of weft threads after which the movements of weft threads repeat.
- **Weave Repeat**: A complete element of the weave.

Shift

- Shift is the distance from a painted square on a thread to its corresponding painted square on its adjacent thread.
- The shift can be counted in warp way, S_o, and in weft way, S_y, (mostly in warp way)
- The shift can be either positive or negative, depending on the direction of counting. Counting from the left to right or from low to high gives positive shift.

Weaving Plan

Weaving Plan consists of Design, Draft plan and Peg plan or Lifting plan

- Draft indicates the number of healds used to produce a given design and the order in which the warp ends are threaded through the eyes of the healds.
- Healds are also called as shafts, leaves, staves, cambs and heddles.
- The basic principle in drafting is that ends which work in different order require separate healds i.e., separate healds for ends working differently and same healds for ends working alike.
- Number of weft yarns has no consequence on draft but should be considered for lifting plan.

Lifting Plan

- Lifting plan (weaving or **pegging plan**) defines the selection of healds to be raised or lowered on each successive insertion of the pick or weft.
- Lifting plan placed along side weave indicate order in which healds are raised and depressed in forming the design.
- The numbered vertical spaces of vertical spaces of lifting plans correspond with the numbers at the side of the drafts.
- Vertical space numbered 1 shows how first heald is operated; numbered two shows that of second heald and so on.
- It further shows which healds are raised and depressed in the succeeding picks.
- In a straight draft lifting plan is same as design.

Weave/Design

- Depends on the order of drafting in the healds combined with the order of lifting or lowering of the healds

DRAFTS AND LIFTING PLANS
Methods of indicating drafts and Lifting plans
By ruling lines:-

- Horizontal lines represent healds
- Vertical lines represent warp threads
- Marks at the intersection indicate the healds upon which the respective threads are drawn

By the use of design paper;-

- Horizontal spaces represent healds
- Vertical spaces represent warp threads
- Marks on the small squares indicate the healds upon which the respective threads are drawn.

By numbering:-

- Numbers below the design refer to the number of healds
- Threads drawn on the healds in the order indicated by the numbers

Relations between Design, Draft And Lifting Plan

- These three elements are closely dependent on one another.
- If any two elements of the weaving plan are known, the third element can be constructed.

Construction of Drafts And Lifting Plans From Given Design

- In a design the threads which are raised and depressed simultaneously may be drawn on the same heald
- The threads that are different from each other must be drawn on different healds.
- As many healds are required as there are threads working differently from each other

Steps in constructing a draft plan and lifting plan are:

i. The first end is indicated on first heald.
ii. All warp yarns with same interlacement are indicated on first heald.
iii. The second end is indicated on second heald
iv. All warp yarns with same interlacement of second warp are indicated on second heald and so on.
v. The working of the first heald is copied from the first vertical space of the design to the first vertical space of the lifting plan.
vi. In constructing the lifting plan healds are taken in succession from front to back.
vii. In a lifting plan,
viii. Vertical spaces = no. of healds in the draft (no of rows in the draft plan)
ix. Horizontal spaces = No of picks in the design.

Construction of Drafts From Given Designs And Lifting Plans

- In a draft number of horizontal spaces = number of vertical spaces in the lifting plan
- Number of vertical spaces = number of warp yarns in the design.
- All the threads of the design which correspond to the interlacement of first vertical space in the lifting plan are drawn on the same heald.

- All the threads of the design which correspond to the interlacement of second vertical space in the lifting plan are drawn on the next heald and so on.

Construction of Design From Given Draft And Lifting Plan

- Number of rows in the design = number of rows in the peg plan
- Number of columns in the design = number of columns in the draft plan
- The first vertical space in the peg plan indicate that how the warp yarns that are connected to the first heald shaft is raised and lowered over the weft yarns
- This interlacement is marked in the corresponding columns of the design as per the markings in the first harness.

SYSTEMS OF DRAFTING
Straight

- Commonly used draft and simplest of all the types of draft plans
- Drafting order progresses successively from first to the last heald frame i.e. first end through first heald, second through the second heald and so on.
- Peg or lifting plan is same as the design

Skip and sateen

- Suitable for weaving fabrics having heavy warp thread density.
- Number of heald frames may be twice or more than the minimum required for a weave
- Purpose is to distribute the warp threads more uniformly to prevent abrasion of threads due to over crowding.

Pointed

- Similar to straight draft
- Suitable for weaves such pointed twill, diamond weaves and ordinary types of honeycombs
- Straight draft is reversed after half the repeat warp way

Herringbone and broken

- Resembles a pointed draft but pointed effect is broken
- Suitable for weaves such as herringbone twill

Herringbone weave

Divided

- Used for weaving two series of warp threads such as terry, double cloth, etc
- Two sets of warp threads divided into groups

Grouped

- Employed for production of stripe and check designs in which stripes have different weaves or their combination
- Repeat of draft is determined by the number of stripes and number of threads in each stripe

- The number of shafts in the draft depends on the number of stripes and the warp repeat of weave of each stripe.

Curved

- Curved draft is used for the production of curved twills

Combined

- Two or more types of draft applied simultaneously. Eg., straight and sateen draft combined
- Combined draft is most complicated and chosen only if there are some technological or economical reasons

Denting

- Drawing ends through a space-dent or split-between two wires in the reed
- If adjacent ends work alike and are drawn through same split of reed they would tend to roll over one another and loss clarity of design.
- Ends which work alike are drawn through different dents to prevent roll over
- If fine dense lines are desired with the ends crammed closely together separated by lines of open fabric, adjacent ends are drawn through same split and one empty dent is left between each filled dent.

Construction of Elementary Weaves
Plain Weave

- Threads interlace in alternate order
- Each thread gives maximum support to adjacent threads
- Texture is stronger and firmer than any other cloth
- They range from canvas, blankets to cambric/muslin
- Trade names are tabby, calico, taffeta
- Variety may be produced by:

a. Threads which are different in colour, material, thickness, or twist or combination of them
b. The number of threads per split of the reed
c. No of picks in a given space is varied in succeeding portions of the cloth
d. The ends are brought from 2 or more warp beams which they are alternately slackened and tightened
e. By the process of dyeing, printing and finishing
f. Rib or cord effects in plain weave is formed if there is considerable difference between the warp and weft threads with to regards thickness

and number per unit space

g. Cords are ribs which run in length of the cloth

h. If number of ends per unit space is greater than that of weft warp rib structure results.

Warp Rib

- Extension of plain weave vertically grouping together several picks in the same shed result in warp rib
- Regular warp rib is produced when each end passes alternatively over and under 2, 3 or 4 picks. Ends are brought prominently to the surface on both sides of the fabric, Line or ribs that are equal in size are formed running the width of the cloth
- Irregular warp ribs produce horizontal lines that are unequal in size. One set of ends are mostly on the surface and the other set are mostly in the back.
- Cloths produced are grosgrain, matelasse.

Weft Rib

- Extension of plain weave horizontally
- In regular weft ribs each pick passes alternately under and over 2,3,or 4 ends
- Weft is brought prominently to the surface and forms lines running the length of the cloth on both sides

Hopsack/Mat/Basket

- Hopsack weaves are constructed by extending the plain weave both vertically and horizontally
- Regular hopsacks are woven with the same number of ends and picks and the same yarn count. Equal warp floats exchange with equal weft floats

Different units of hopsack are arranged in one repeat, with the distribution of warp or weft floats being equal or a predominance of either

Mock Rib

- Weaves produced in plain weave which resemble warp rib or weft rib
- Mock warp rib is achieved by doubling up two threads of weft in a pirn inserting double weft in lieu of 2 single picks in warp rib construction
- Mock weft rib effect is obtained in plain weave by placing two ends in each mail
- If these two threads are differently coloured the rolling of the threads takes place and causes colours to show intermittently in the cloth.

Twill Weave

- The most characteristic of twill is that they have diagonal lines on the cloth.
- The twill weaves are expressed in the form of a fraction such as 3/1, 1/3, 2/1, 4/1

- Provides greater weight, closer setting and better draping quality than plain weave formed with similar yarn

In simple twills points of intersection move one outward and one upward

- Can be made with more than 2 threads
- Twill line is formed on both sides of the cloth
- Direction of lines either to right or to left
- Direction on one side of fabric is opposite to the other when cloth is turned over
- If warp prominent on one side weft will be prominent on the other.

Warp Faced Twills
In these types of twills the warp thread floats over all the picks in a repeat except one pick. The minimum repeat size required is 3. Examples of warp faced twills are 2/1, 3/1, 4/1, 5/1 etc.
Weft Faced Twills
These twills are the reverse of the previous ones. In these weaves the weft thread floats over the warp on all picks in a repeat except one. Examples of weft faced twills are 1/2, 1/3, 1/4, 1/5 etc.
Balanced and Unbalanced Twills

In these types of twills the warp and weft floats may be equal or unequal. In other words the twills may be of the reversible or irreversible types. Accordingly they may be known as balanced and unbalanced twills. Examples of balanced twills are 2/2, 3/3, 4/4, 5/5 etc.

Examples of unbalanced twills are 2/3, 4/2, 5/3 etc. The 2/2 twill is popularly known as "Gaberdene" weave. A and B show designs for balanced and unbalanced twills and C and D show the interlacement diagrams of a 4/1 twill and ¼ twill (warp faced) (weft faced).

Designation of Twills

- Twills are designated by describing the interlacing of the first thread 2 up & 2 down or 2- and -2 or 2/2.
- It means on the first pick first two ends are up and following 2 down or on the first end first two picks are down and following 2 up.
- twill gives a repeat of 4 ends and 4 picks
- Warp faced twill shows more number of warp on the face and greater number of ends per cm than picks per cm. Eg 3/1 twill
- Weft faced twill shows more number of weft on the face and greater number of picks per cm than ends per cm. Eg 1/3 twill
- ½ or 2/1 is called cashmere, jean, jeanette and genoa
- 1/3 or 2/2 called serge, blanket, sheeting or shalloon. 3/1 commonly called drill.
- Large twills commonly known as diagonals

Prominence of twill

The effect of using all of the twist combinations for this weave is given below. For a Z twill fabric.

- S twist warp × Z twist weft = prominent twill
- S twist warp × S twist weft = warp twill prominent
- Z twist warp × Z twist weft = weft twill prominent
- Z twist warp × S twist weft = twill indistinct

The following factors determine the relative prominence of twill weaves
(*i*) Nature of the yarn
(*ii*) Nature of the weave
(*iii*) The warp and weft threads/inch, and
(*iv*) The relative direction of twill and yarn twist

Types of Twills
Waved Twills/ Pointed Twills

- Formed by reversing the direction of the twill at suitable intervals
- Reversal on a warp thread produce horizontal weave and weft thread produces a vertical wave or zig-zag effect
- Horizontal weave produced in point drafts and vertical weave using dobby shedding motion.

A defect of pointed twill arrangement is the formation of an increased float where the weave turns

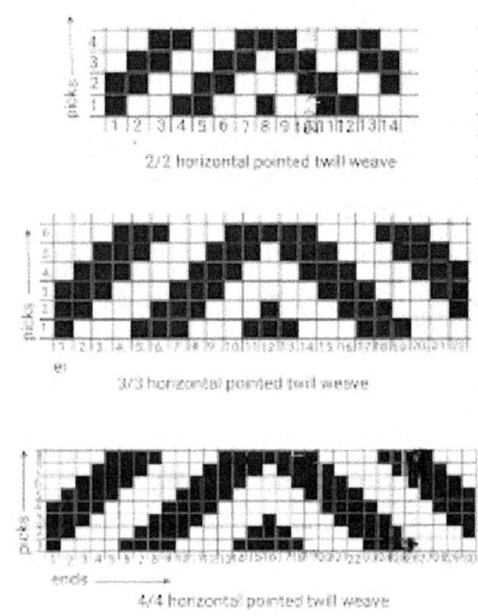

2/2 horizontal pointed twill weave

3/3 horizontal pointed twill weave

4/4 horizontal pointed twill weave

Waved Twill

Herringbone Twills

- These also depend upon the reversal of the direction
- The twill does not come to a point where it changes the direction but instead one twill line is cut into the other at the point of reversal.
- The effect of diametrically opposite lifts at the reversal point throw the neighboring ends from one anther producing a break or cut.
- This tends to produce a distinct stripe effect and prevent formation of float that is seen in waved twill.

Curved Twills

- The curved twill weaves are constructed on the basis of curved draft.
- Main disadvantage is that the length of the weft float and the firmness of the cloth vary in different parts of twill line.
- Curved twills may be reversed in direction forming zig-zag effects or undulating weave twill may be made.

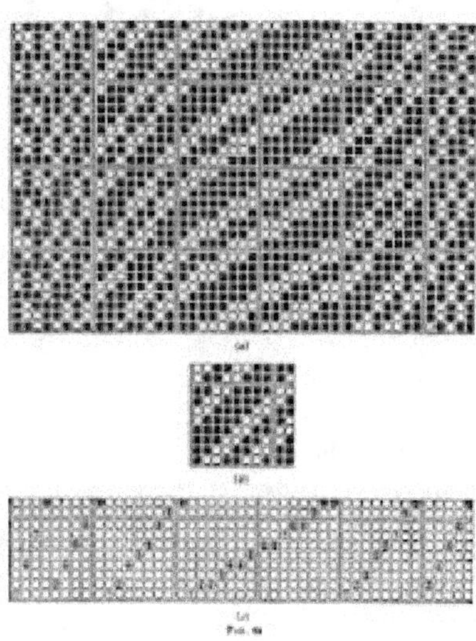

Curved Weave

Broken Twills

- The break can be achieved in different ways by stopping the continuity of the twill through frequent reversals of direction.
- Orderly progression of regular twill stopped in half-way through the repeat and running the ends in second half of the repeat in reverse order. For eg; In the eight thread twill the drafting order is 1,2,3,4/8,7,6,5.

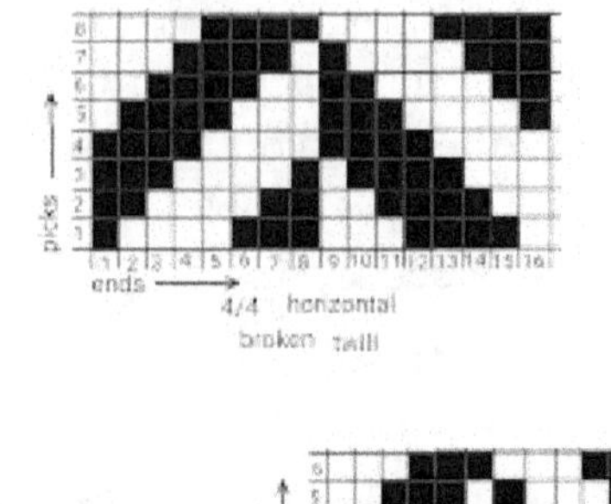

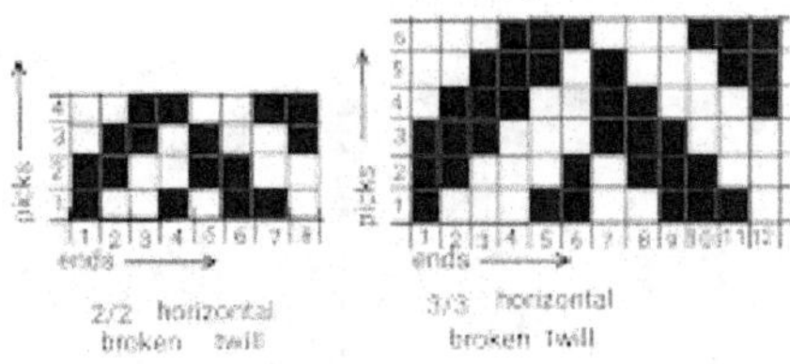

Broken Weave

- 1 X 3 broken twill is called 'Satinette'
- Draft can be broken in pairs .1,2/4,3;5,6/8,7.
- For twills with equal warp and weft float "entering and skipping" the threads of ordinary twill can be done.

- Broken draft is suitable for herringbone and broken twills

Transposed or Rearranged Twills

- New and attractive designs can be created by transposition or re-arrangement.
- Some transposed effects are similar to broken twill

Elongated Twills

- The angle formed in the cloth by a twill weave depends upon

  1. The relative ratio of ends and picks per unit space
  2. The rate of advance of one interlacing in respect of the following one

- If there more ends than picks per inch, the line of an ordinary twill more nearly approaches the vertical; while if the picks exceed the ends the line becomes flatten
- Relationship between angled formed by the twill and the number of threads is given by

$$\tan \alpha = \frac{\underline{\text{Rate of advancement of twill upwards}}}{\text{Rate of advancement of twill outwards}} \times \frac{\underline{\text{ends per cm}}}{\text{picks per cm}}$$

- Steep twills which produce distinct twill lines of warp in the cloth are termed 'whip cords.

Combination of Twills

- Designs created by combining small ordinary twill in the order of an end or a pick of each alternatively
- If the weave repeat of two twills differ then the LCM of both should be taken.

Satin and Sateen Weaves

- The characteristic of the sateen/satin weave is that they have a smoothness and lustrous fabric surface.
- Surface of cloth consists almost entirely either of warp or weft
- In the repeat of a weave each thread of one series passes over all but one thread of the other series
- Interlacing points are so arranged as to allow the floating threads to slip and to cover the binding point of one thread by the float of another.
- This results in fabrics with a maximum degree of smoothness and luster without any prominent weave features
- Fabrics with insufficiently close thread spacing exhibit poor seam strength due to seam slippage

- It has no prominent twill line

Difference between Sateen and satin

- Sateen indicates a weft faced construction where as satin refers to corresponding warp faced construction
- Sateen is constructed with greater number of pick per cm than ends per cm where as satin have more ends than picks per cm to achieve desired solid effect
- Sateen weaves have a weft effect with weft float and satin weaves have a warp effect with warp float.

Construction of sateen and satin weaves

- The sateen weave is denoted by a fraction. Numerator is equal to the repeat of the weave and the denominator equals shift or move of overlaps.

- First weave represent 5/3 (5 end sateen with move or shift number 3) sateen. They are also called 5 ends (or shafts) sateen.
- Second weave represent 7/3 (7 end sateen with move or shift number 3) sateen. they are also called 7 ends(or shafts) sateen
- Third weave represent 5/2 (5 end satin with move or shift number 2) satin.
- And they are also called 5 ends(5 shafts) sateen and 7 ends (7 shafts) sateen

Regular Sateen and Satins

- In twill weaves the distance from a mark on one thread to the corresponding mark on the next thread-termed step, move or count is one. So distinct twill lines are formed
- In regular sateen/satin weaves the step is more than one, but as the distance moved each time is equal and regular a certain degree of twilling is formed in the cloth
- The prominence of twill line varies according to

  1. The order in which threads interlace
  2. The direction of twill line in relation to direction of twist of the yarn i.e. if the twill lines and the twist run in the same direction, a smooth, lustrous and almost un-twilled surface is formed

Rules for construction regular Sateen/Satin weaves

- The move number:

a. Should not be equal to the repeat of the weave.
b. Should not be one less than the repeat size.
c. should not be a factor of the repeat size
d. should not be a multiple of the factor
e. Should not be equal to one

Irregular Sateen And Satins

- Regular sateens or satins cannot be constructed on 4 and 6 threads
- Irregular sateens are entirely free from twill lines. It gives an advantage over regular sateens
- In an irregular eight thread sateen,

i. for the first 4 picks 3 is counted to the right ;
ii. On the fifth pick count is equal to half the number of threads in the repeat i.e. 4
iii. On the succeeding picks 3 is counted to the left.

Simple Developments

- In simple derivatives the new design is built up by using the original satin or sateen as the base and subtracting or adding marks as required in the same relative position to each base mark.
- Various structures in this class are known by the name swansdown, lambskin, imperial etc.
- Venetian weave and buckskin weave are two main weaves under this category.

Extension of Sateen Weaves

- Sateen weaves may be extended horizontally, vertically or both horizontally and vertically
- Their chief value is that with the same number of healds longer floats are formed on the surface of the cloth than in the case with ordinary sateen

- Satin base can be equally used but as the development by subtraction of marks is rather more difficult the sateen weaves are generally preferred on the grounds of convenience.

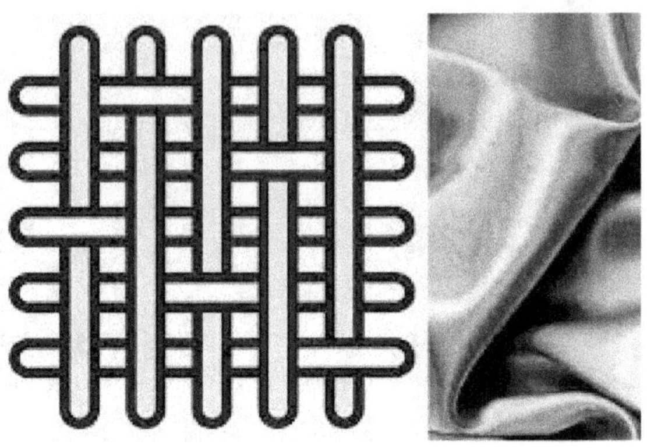

Satin Weave

POINTS TO REMEMBER

- **Woven fabrics** are composed of longitudinal warp threads and transverse weft threads interlaced with one another according to the class of structure and form of design that is desired.
- Warp threads are individually known as **ends.** Weft threads are individually known as **picks** or **filling.**
- The number of heald shafts depends on the warp repeat of the weave. It is decided by the drafting plan of a weave.
- The sley mechanism swings to and fro. It is responsible for pushing the last pick of weft to the fell of the cloth by means of the beat up motion.
- **Shuttle** is basically a weft carrier and helps in interlacement of the weft with the warp threads to form cloth.
- **Picker sustains** the force of the shuttle while entering the box.
- **Warp beam** is also known as the weaver's beam.
- **Breast beam** is also known as the front rest & maintain proper tension to facilitate weaving.
- **Back beam** is also known as the back rest.**Cloth beam** is also known as the cloth roller. The woven cloth is wound on to this roller.

- **Shedding** is the heart of weaving as it determines the nature of interlacing or the weave.
- Canvas Method using design paper also called point paper or squared paper.
- **Draft** indicates the number of healds used to produce a given design and the order in which the warp ends are threaded through the eyes of the healds.
- Healds are also called as shafts, leaves, staves, cambs and heddles.
- **Lifting plan** (weaving or **pegging plan**) defines the selection of healds to be raised or lowered on each successive insertion of the pick or weft.
- Extension of plain weave vertically grouping together several picks in the same shed result in **warp rib.**
- Extension of plain weave horizontally is known as **weft rib.**
- **Hopsack** weaves are constructed by extending the plain weave both vertically and horizontally. The 2/2 twill is popularly known as **"Gaberdene" weave.**

SUGGESTED QUESTIONS:

SECTION A

1. The 2/2 twill is popularly known as ___________ weave.
2. ___________ defines the selection of healds to be raised or lowered on each successive insertion of the pick or weft.
3. ___________ are also called as shafts, leaves, staves, cambs and heddles.
4. ___________ is the heart of weaving as it determines the nature of interlacing or the weave.
5. ___________ weaves are constructed by extending the plain weave both vertically and horizontally.
6. Warp threads are individually known as ___________.
7. Weft threads are individually known as ___________.
8. ___________ indicates the number of healds used to produce a given design and the order in which the warp ends are threaded through the eyes of the healds.
9. Define weaving.
10. ___________ is basically a weft carrier and helps in interlacement of the weft with the warp threads to form cloth.

SECTION B

1. Give the elements of woven design
2. Explain the methods of fabric representation
3. Explain draft and lifting plans
4. Briefly describe the construction of elementary weaves
5. Describe the construction of plain weaves and their derivatives

SECTION C

1. Explain the construction of warp rib and their derivatives
2. Briefly describe the construction of weft rib and their derivatives
3. Describe the construction of twill and their derivatives
4. Briefly describe the modification of twills and their derivatives
5. Describe the construction of satin and sateen weaves and their derivatives

CHAPTER II

Modified Weave

AIMS & OBJECTIVES

The main aim of this chapter is to study the Ordinary and Brighten honey comb , Huck a back Crepe weaves, Mock leno and its modifications.

Honeycomb Weaves

- The honey comb weaves derive their name from their partial resemblance to the hexagonal honey comb cells of wax in which bees store their honey.
- Threads form ridges and hollows giving cell-like appearance to the textures
- Both warp and weft threads floats some what freely on both sides and has rough structure making it readily absorbent to moisture
- Used for towels, bed covers and quilts.
- There are two classes

Ordinary Honeycomb Weaves

- Give similar effect on both sides of fabric
- They can be woven in pointed draft

Steps in construction

- A pointed draft is indicated on required number of healds.
- Then marks are reversed.
- One of the diamond space is filled in while others left blank.

AIMS & OBJECTIVES

The main aim of this chapter is to study the Ordinary and Brighten honey comb , Huck a back Crepe weaves, Mock leno and its modifications.

Honeycomb Weaves

- The honey comb weaves derive their name from their partial resemblance to the hexagonal honey comb cells of wax in which bees store their honey.

- Threads form ridges and hollows giving cell-like appearance to the textures
- Both warp and weft threads floats some what freely on both sides and has rough structure making it readily absorbent to moisture
- Used for towels, bed covers and quilts.
- There are two classes

Ordinary Honeycomb Weaves

- Give similar effect on both sides of fabric
- They can be woven in pointed draft

Steps in construction

- A pointed draft is indicated on required number of healds.
- Then marks are reversed.
- One of the diamond space is filled in while others left blank.

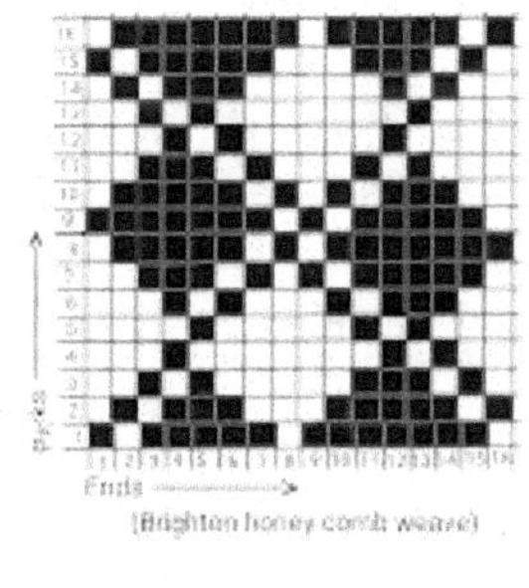

(Brighton honey comb weave)

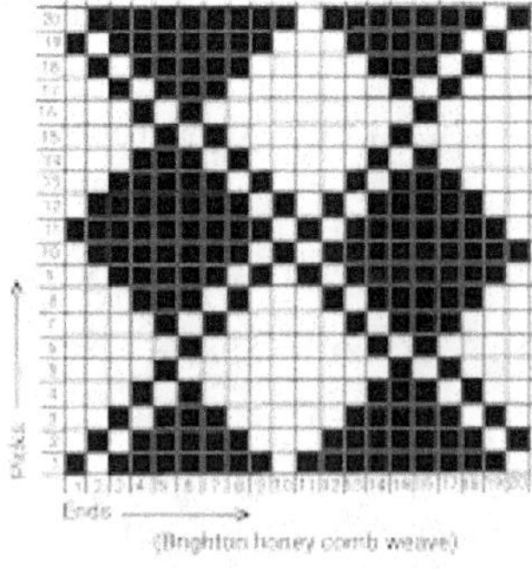

(Brighton honey comb weave)

Honeycomb Weave

- Warp ridge formed by first end and weft ridge by the first pick.
- Plain weave about the center of the design tightens the thread and cause depression to be formed.
- Cellular formation makes the pattern appear rectangular in the cloth although weave are constructed in diamond basis.
- Warp ridge formed by first end and weft ridge by the first pick.
- Plain weave about the center of the design tightens the thread and cause depression to be formed.
- Cellular formation makes the pattern appear rectangular in the cloth although weave are constructed in diamond basis.

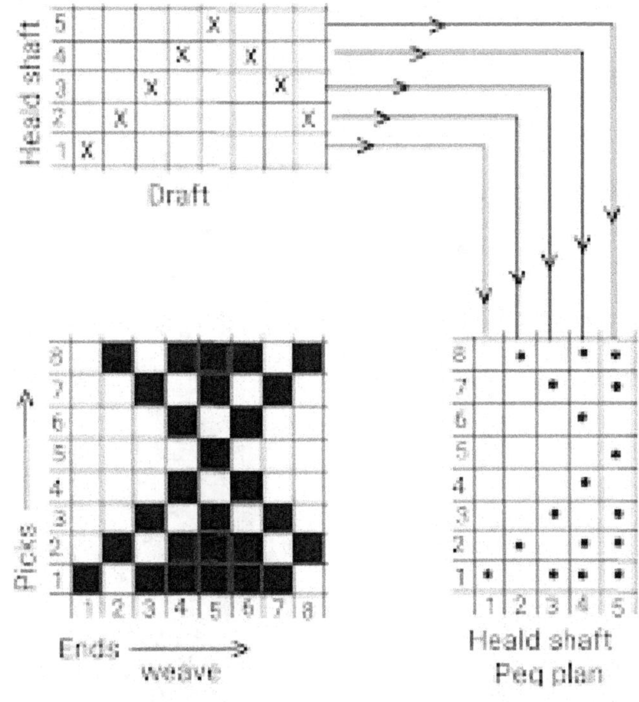

Honeycomb weave pattern

Brighton Honeycomb Weaves

- It is woven in straight drafts.
- Number of threads in the repeat should be a multiple of 4

Steps in construction

- Diamond base is first made by inserting a single row of marks in one direction and a double row in the other direction
- Marks are then added to double rows so as to form a small warp diamond in the right and left corners of each diamond space.

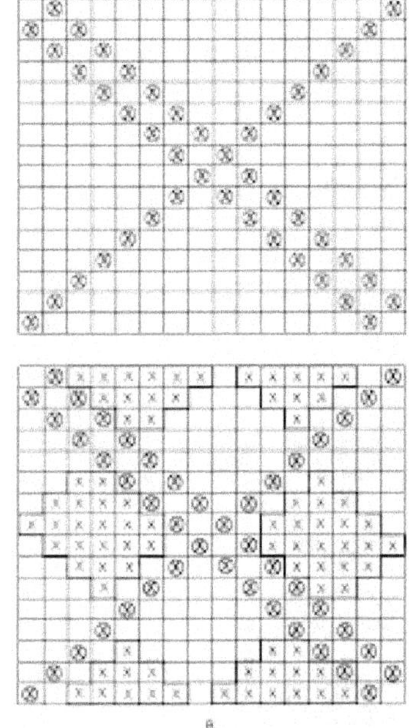

Brighton Honeycomb

- Similar weft diamond is formed in upper and lower corner.
- Long centre floats of warp and weft form horizontal and vertical ridges.
- Two sizes of hollows are formed.

- In ordinary honey comb each repeat forms only one cell.
- Brighton weave produces two large and two small cells.

In the construction of Brighton honey comb weaves, a diamond base is first made by insertion of a single diagonal and then a double diagonal to cross it. Suitable motifs as shown in figure above are inserted inside the spaces of the diagonals. It is to be remembered that the length of the longest float in the motif should not exceed $(N/2 - 1)$, where N is the size of the repeat of the weave.

Huck a back

- The huck a back weaves are basically toweling fabrics .
- They are constructed by alternately combining a floating with a plain weave. Interestingly, a number of weaves are derived from these weaves.
- Huck a back weaves are suitable for producing thick and heavy textures.
- One of the well known heavier varieties of this class is the "Grecians".
- The design of huck a back weaves permits stripe and check effects to be brought out in the fabrics.
- The huck a back weaves are generally characterized by the following features:

1. Repeat is divided into four equal parts. Two parts are filled with plain weave and remaining two parts are filled with long float motif.
2. Plain weave gives firmness to the cloth.
3. Long float motif gives moisture absorbency.

- The loom equipment required would ideally be a dobby loom fitted with a fast reed mechanism
- Used for Linen, cotton towels, glass-cloths.
- Areas of plain weave give firmness and hard wearing qualities while areas of loose floats provide good moisture pick up.
- 6 pick huck a back weave is called as devon huck.

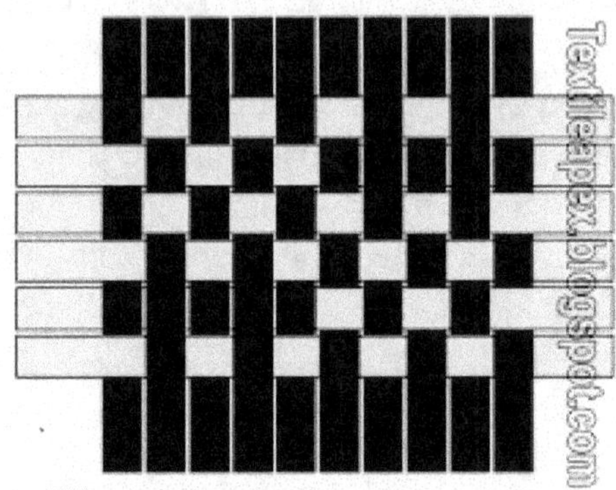

Enter Caption

- Design which repeats upon a larger number of threads and contain longer floats is termed as honeycomb-huckaback.

CREPE WEAVES

Crepe weaves constitute an useful variety of simple weaves and are also known as "crape" or "oatmeal" fabrics due to their pebbly or crinkled (rough) surface. The size of the pebbles and their arrangement on the fabric surface determine the type of crepe fabric.

The crepe effect can be achieved either by the use of crepe yarns (highly twisted) or a crepe weave, and sometimes by special process of finishing, i.e., embossing. Crepe weaves are commonly used in combination with other elementary weaves, to produce a variety of various effects in elaborate jacquard designs for brocade and related fabrics.

- Crepe weaves contain little or no twilled or other prominent effect
- It give the appearance of being covered by minute spots or seeds
- These constructions are also known as oat meal weaves
- This is not same as crepe cloths (formed by high twist yarns)

Construction of Crepe Weaves Upon Sateen Bases
By adding marks in certain orders to some of sateen marks

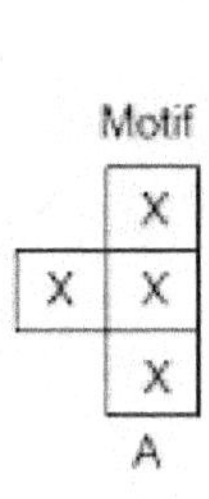

Crepe Weave

At Fig. A, is shown the base sateen weave and at Fig. B, is shown the crepe effect obtained by insertion of a twill weave (3/1 and 1/3) upon the sateen base. The sateen weave has been marked with a different notation in order to identify the base weave.

Combination of Floating Weaves With Plain Thread

- Threads that work plain are combined with threads of a floating weave which are arranged in a sateen order

Steps in construction

- Plain marks are indicated in odd ends

- Sateen marks (satinette) are added on alternate picks of the even ends

- Marks are then added to the sateen base marks in an order which fits with the plain weave.

Crepe Weaves Produced By Reversing

- Reversing principle of constructing designs is employed
Weaves containing minute floats can be built up to this base.

Insertion of One Weave Over Another

- This weave is formed by inserting two different weaves one over the other
- To produce irregular effect at least one of the weaves or both should be irregular. Eg. Satinette and derivatives of eight end Sateen.
- Weaves containing minute floats can be built up to this base.

Mock Leno

Mock lenos, also known as imitation lenos are a variety of weaves of ordinary construction which produce effects that are similar in appearance to the gauze or leno styles obtained with the aid of doup mounting. These weaves are generally produced in combination with a plain, twill, satin or other simple weaves or even with brocade figuring, to produce striped fabrics, which bear a very close resemblance to true leno fabrics. Two kinds of structures are produced by the weaves,

(*i*) Perforated fabrics which imitate open gauze effects

(*ii*) Distorted thread effects which imitate spider or net leno styles

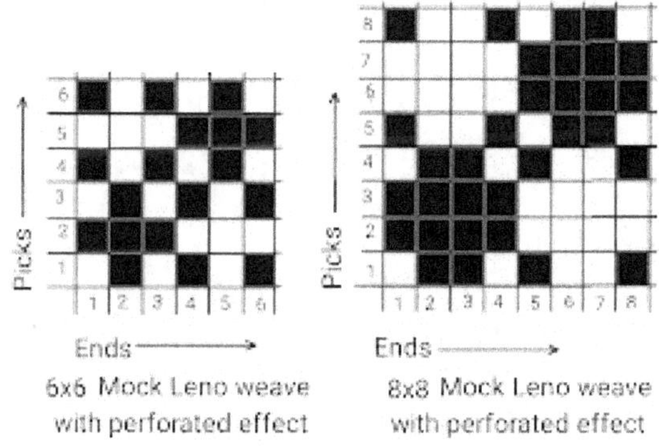

6x6 Mock Leno weave with perforated effect

8x8 Mock Leno weave with perforated effect

Mock Leno Weave

Perforated Fabrics

- It forms an imitation of open gauze effects.
- Each weave is constructed by reversing a small unit
- Warp threads run in groups with a space between and are crossed by weft threads which are grouped together in a similar manner
- Open appearance of the cloth can be improved or obscured by the system of denting i.e. if each group of ends is passed through a separate

split the reed assorts in drawing the thread together in groups.

- Open appearance can be further enhanced by using fine reed and missing alternate splits.
- Open gauze weaves are used for canvas cloths, window curtains, dress fabrics, blouses, aprons etc or in combination with other weave.
- Imitation of open leno effects obtained in plain weave by missing splits in the reed.

Distorted Thread Effects

- It forms an imitation of spider or net leno styles.
- Imitation gauze weaves of this class may be arranged to distort certain threads in either the weft or the warp or in both weft and warp.

Steps in construction

- The ground structure is plain weave.
- Construct a point paper with 14 X 14.
- The forth and eleventh ends which are distorted float over all the plain picks but pass under fourth and 11th pick.
- The fourth and eleventh picks float over one group of plain ends and under the next group in alternate order.
- They are drawn towards each other where the picks 4 and 11 float over the ground ends.
- Open appearance can be further enhanced by using fine reed and missing alternate splits.
- Open gauze weaves are used for canvas cloths, window curtains, dress fabrics, blouses, aprons etc or in combination with other weave.
- Imitation of open leno effects obtained in plain weave by missing splits in the reed.

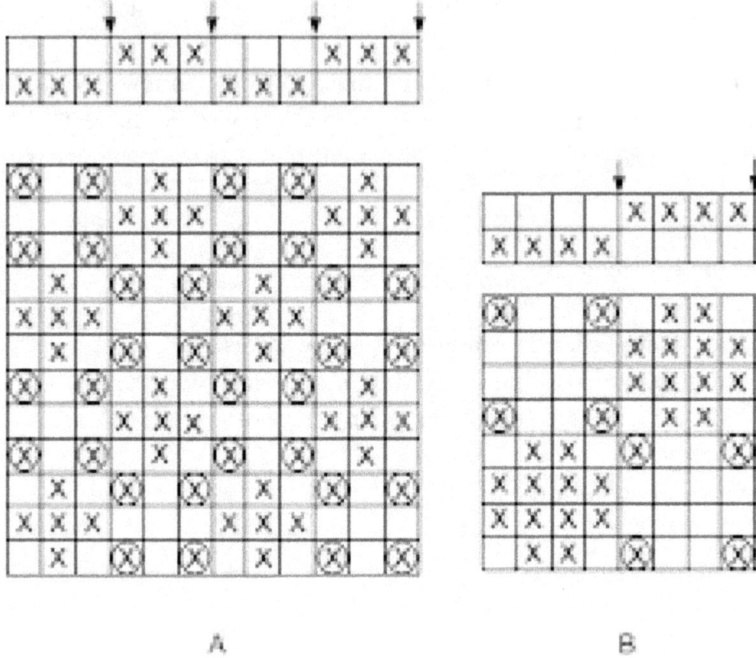

Mock Leno

POINTS TO REMEMBER

- The honey comb weaves derive their name from their partial resemblance to the hexagonal honey comb cells of wax in which bees store their honey.
- **Ordinary Honeycomb Weaves** give similar effect on both sides of fabric
- The huck a back weaves are basically towelling fabrics .
- Huck a back weaves are suitable for producing thick and heavy textures.
- One of the well known heavier varieties of huck a back is the "Grecians".
- The design of huck a back weaves permits stripe and check effects to be brought out in the fabrics.
- 6 pick huck a back weave is called as devon huck.
- Design which repeats upon a larger number of threads and contain longer floats is termed as honeycomb-huckaback.

- Mock leno weaves are generally produced in combination with a plain, twill, satin or other simple weaves or even with brocade figuring, to produce striped fabrics, which bear a very close resemblance to true leno fabrics.
- Crepe weaves constitute an useful variety of simple weaves and are also known as "crape" or "oatmeal" fabrics due to their pebbly or crinkled (rough) surface.
- The crepe effect can be achieved either by the use of crepe yarns (highly twisted) or a crepe weave, and sometimes by special process of finishing, i.e., embossing.
- In honeycomb ,Both warp and weft threads floats some what freely on both sides and has rough structure making it readily absorbent to moisture

SUGGESTED QUESTIONS:

SECTION A

1. _____________ weavesgive similar effect on both sides of fabric.
2. _________ weaves are suitable for producing thick and heavy textures.
3. One of the well known heavier varieties of huck a back is the _____________.
4. 6 pick huck a back weave is called as____________.
5. ___________ are also known as "crape" or "oatmeal" fabrics.
7. Design which repeats upon a larger number of threads and contain longer floats is termed as ____________.

SECTION B

1.Explain Ordinary honey comb weave .
2.Give an account on Brighton honey comb,
3.Explain Huck a back .
4.Write about crepe weave.
5.Write about mock leno.

SECTION C

6.Explain Ordinary honey comb weave and its modification
7.Explain Brighton honey comb and its modification,
8.Explain Huck a back and its modifications
9.Write about crepe weaves
10.Write about mock leno.

CHAPTER III

Extra Warp & Weft

AIMS & OBJECTIVES

The main aim of this chapter is to study the Extra warp and extra weft figuring – single and two colours, planting, backed fabric, warp and weft backed fabrics.

FIGURING WITH EXTRA THREADS

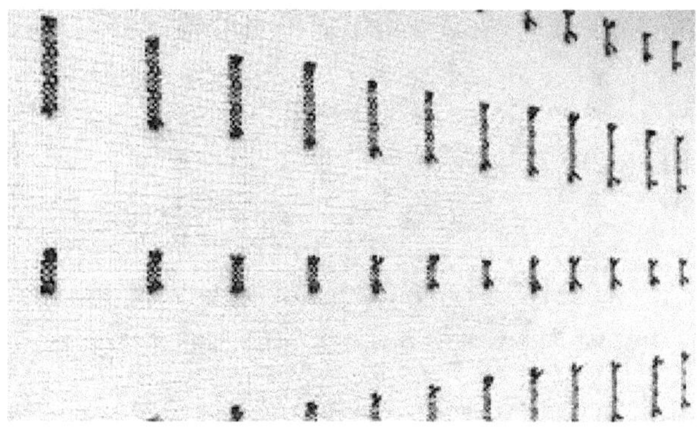

Extra Warp or Weft

Principles of Figuring With Extra Materials

- Distinguishing feature of figuring with extra thread is that withdrawal of extra threads from the cloth leaves a complete ground structure under the figure.
- Formation of figure by means of extra threads does not affect the strength or wearing quality of the fabric.
- The main advantages of figuring with extra materials are

- Bright colours in sharp contrast with ground may be brought to the surface of the cloth in any desired proportion

- Pleasing colour combinations can be obtained
  ### Methods of Introducing Extra Figuring Threads

42

- Extra threads may be introduced either as weft or warp or in a combination of warp and weft
- For extra warp figuring- a separate warp beam is required for each warp on account of the different take up rates between the extra and the ground ends.
- For extra weft figuring- The weaving machine must have the capacity to insert more than one colour or kind of weft.
- The extra threads may be inserted in continuous order or in intermittent order.
- The arrangement of the figuring and ground threads may be 1- and -1, 1- and -2, 1- and -3, etc. according to the structure of the cloth and solidity of figure required

Methods of Disposing of the Surplus Threads

- The disposal of the extra warp or weft threads in the portions of the cloth where they are not required to form the figure is essential.
- Any one of the following methods are adopted for the same
- Extra yarn is allowed to float loosely on the back in the ground of the cloth.
- This method is suitable when the space between the figures is not excessive or when the ground is dense.
- It is not applicable to the cloths in which the ground is so light and transparent that the position of the extra threads on the back is visible from face side.
- The extra yarn is allowed to float loosely on the back, and is afterwards cut away.
- This method is suitable for light ground textures.
- If the extra threads float somewhat loosely on the surface in forming the ornament, it is necessary for them to be bound in at edges of the figure by interweaving, or the loose figuring floats will fray out from the surface.
- However the firm interweaving of the extra yarns at the edge makes the outline of the figure less distinct.
- In compact fabrics the extra threads are bound in on the underside of the cloth either between corresponding floats in the ground texture or by means of special stitching threads.

- The extra threads are interwoven on the face of the cloth in the form of small auxiliary figures or floats thus adding the fullness of the texture.

Comparison of Extra Warp with Extra Weft Figuring
Extra Warp Figuring

- Productivity of loom is greater because only one series of pick is inserted
- Faster running loom can be used
- No special picking box and uptake motions required
- There is no limit to the number of colors that can be introduced
- Intermittent spotted or stripe patterns can be formed
- Two or more warp beams are required
- In dobby weaving the drafts are more complicated
- Stronger yarns are required for the figuring so the threads are not soft, full and lustrous
- Extra warp effects show less prominently
- It is costlier to cut away the extra threads from underside.

Extra Weft Figuring

- Special drop box mechanism required.
- No. of colors that can be introduced is limited
- Productivity of loom is comparatively less due to insertion of more picks
- Only one warp beam is required
- Stripe patterns are not possible due to objectionable appearance of horizontal lines.
- Figuring threads need not be much stronger as they are not under much tension
- Extra weft figuring effects are more stronger than extra warp figuring effects
- Cost of cutting away the surplus thread underside is comparatively less.

EXTRA WARP FIGURING

- It is mostly utilized for continuous styles arranged one end of ground and one end of extra
- There is a decline of fancier jacquard stripe styles because

1. Each different design frequently requires the harness to be re-tied or modified which is costly in itself
2. It often leads to further costs by increasing the length of weaving machine down time
3. Additional costs are incurred by the need to draw-in new warps than in knotting in.
4. Many elaborate styles similar in appearance to extra warp can be produced by means of extra weft figuring using standard harness setts.

Continuous Figuring in One Extra Warp

- In an extra warp figured fabric in which the ends may be arranged continuously in the order of 1 extra and 1 ground the extra ends can be floated on the back during weaving.
- In some types these extra ends floated on the back are cut away in the finishing process.
- In some other types the figure is stitched at the edges which soften the outline of the figure and then the floats at the back are cut away.
- Figure A shows the weave of ground ends B the extra warp figure

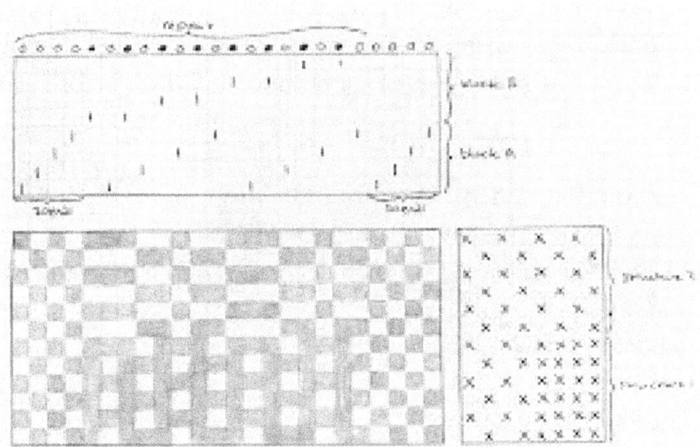

Extra warp figuring

- The red marks indicates the lifts of extra ends which are drawn on the odd harness mails
- The black marks indicates the lifts of ground ends and are drawn on the even harness mails
- If the ground ends and picks per unit space is equal in the cloth and the arrangement is 1 extra and 1 ground, there are twice as many ends as picks per unit space. 16 X 10 design paper is therefore suitable in construction full design in either case.

Binding in Extra Ends between Face Floats

- In the ground of ordinary extra warp figured fabrics, it is necessary to make extra threads to be invisible from the face side.
- They can be floated loosely on the back
- If the ground weave is suitable these extra threads can be bound-in between corresponding warp float.

Intermittent Figuring in One Extra Warp

- Series of extra ends can be introduced intermittently forming stripes or detached figures.

- Denting plan: The ground ends are dented regularly two per dent with figuring ends being added to some dents as they occur, so that in some splits there may be four ends, in some three and in some others only two ground ends.

- Clipped spot effect on an open ground cloth represents dobby styles. If the extra yarn is cut away on the back of the fabric it could be easily plucked from the surface if it was insecurely anchored to the cloth.

- The anchorage can be achieved in two ways

- Ground ends are dented one per dent and where the extra ends occur they are crammed 3 per dents together with the ground end so that they are held between two adjacent ground ends.
- The extra ends are not permitted to float continuously on the surface but are bound in at intervals in such a manner that the binding is not

noticeable.

Figuring With Two Extra Warps

- In fabrics with two extra warp figuring, one extra warp is introduced continuously and second extra warp is introduced intermittently
- First extra warp figuring is used to form what may be termed as the ground pattern while the second assist the first in producing a figure in two colours
- The intermittent extra warp can also be used to form detached spots independent of the other.
- For indication the figure on the design paper first design with both colours are conveniently marked.
- Then the complete plan for the distribution of extra ends is given
- Lastly the full structure including the ground weave is indicated.

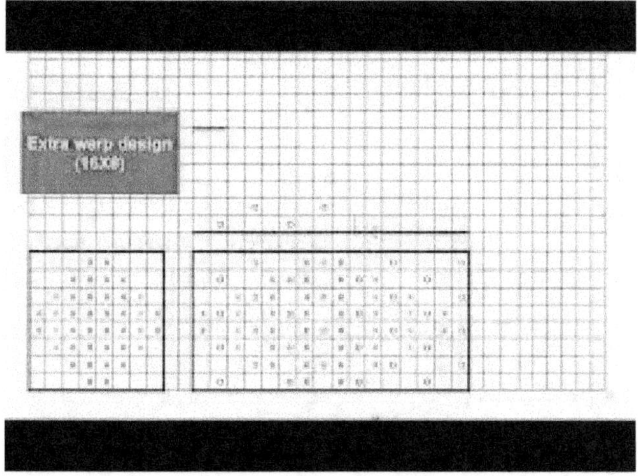

Extra Warp

Extra Warp Planting

- Planting enables a figure to be formed in a large number of colours without an addition being actually made to the series of extra threads.
- But only two colours are introduced in any vertical line of the design
- The number of extra thread in the arrangement is thus equivalent to a two colour extra warp figuring.

EXTRA WEFT FIGURING

- Extra weft figured fabrics are formed with one, two or more extra weft picks in addition to the ground weft.
- Only one series of warp threads is used and the effect is obtained by floating the extra weft where desired on the face of the ground cloth.
- Weaving machines should have capacity to insert more than one kind of weft.
- Extra weft can be inserted continuously or intermittently.

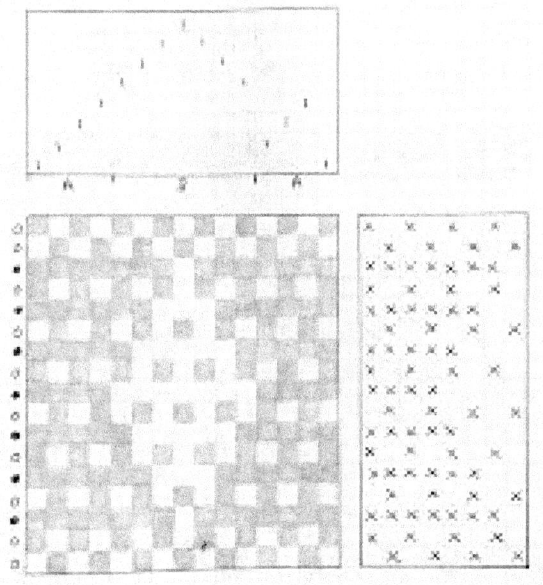

Extra Weft

Continuous Figuring in One Extra Weft

- In continuous figuring in the extra weft is introduced continuously with ground weft in the order of a pick of each alternately.

- The ground ends and picks interweave in plain order which the extra pick float loosely on the back where no figure is formed on the surface.
- The figuring picks are arranged in the order 1:2 with the ground picks which are indicated with different markings.
- The ground weft pick have plain interlacement and the extra picks will have the interlacement according to the extra figure design.
- Greater solidify of the figure is obtained by discontinuity the weave of the ground picks, beneath the extra weft floats i.e. the pick arrangement as one ground 2 extra frequently.
- In some cases the ground weft and the extra weft interweaves each other.

Clipped Spot Effects

- This effect is normally formed in extra weft on a plain transparent ground texture which necessitates extra material be cut off on the underside.
- To prevent fraying out of extra picks they are interweaves in palm order at the sides of frying floats extended completely round so as to produce an opaque outline between the weft figure and then ground texture.
- In the design paper

    - The figure is first painted in solid and
    - Then means are inserted to stop exclusively lay weft floats
    - And later the plain binding is indicated round the figure.
    - Finally the ground pick interlacement is marked between the weft figuring threads based on the ratio.

Intermittent Extra Weft Figuring

- Introducing extra weft in intermittent order produces a detached spot effect.
- Intermittent extra weft figure can be combined with a figure formed by ground weave.
- If the extra weft figure is rendered in long floats and the extra yarn is not cut away from the back of the cloth it has to be stitched on the reverse side to prevent extreme floating.

Chintzing

- Two different colours of extra weft are used in forming different parts of figure.
- The structures was not changed in the principle and still be considered a one extra weft construction.
- Replacement of one colour of extra weft by another in succeeding horizontal rows of design is known as chintzing and it corresponds with warp planting.

Continuous Figuring With Two Extra Wefts

- A continuous figure is developed in 2 colours of extra weft with a pile of each being introduced regularly with each pile of ground weft.
- It is assumed that the EPI and PPI are same for the ground fabric.
- The figuring design alone is first denoted in the point paper with different markings for different colours.
- Then the ground weft first extra weft and second extra weft is marked in horizontal rows in a different ratio say 1- and − 1, 2-and-2
- Two extras can be introduced continuously by denoting the weft in the sequence first ground, first extra, 2nd ground, 2nd extra in consecutively.

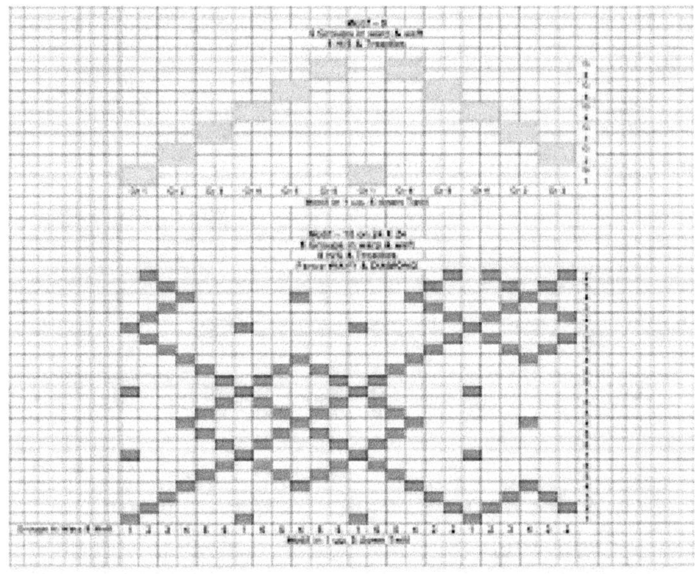

Extra Weft

PLANTING

Without an addition being actually made to the series of extra threads a figure is formed in a large no.of colours .

Absort the given motif in this (ex) 5 colours (represented by different colours) are employed. It will be noted that 2 colours only are introduced in any vertical line of the design. So for as regards the no.of extra threads ,the arrangements is thus equivalent to a 2 coloured extrawarp.The order in which the color replace each often can be observed by the following garment of design.This type of figuring is called **"planting"**.

Backed Cloth

- Backed principle of construction employed for the following purposes

  - To increase the warmth-retaining qualities of a cloth.
  - To obtain any desired weight combined with the five surface appearance of a light single fabric.

- The idea is to employ the threads forming a back to a face fabric.

- One of the advantages of backed construction is that extra weight can be obtained in aneconomical manner, since material which is introduced to the face to the face yarns may be used on the underside.
- These are constructed on both backed weft and backed warp principle.
- Backed weft fabrics consist of two series of weft thread and one series of warp thread.
- Backed warp fabrics consist of two series of warp threads and on series of weft thread

Construction of Design Paper of Backed Fabrics

- Construction of these fabrics on design paper is carried out in several stages.

- Mark out on design paper face threads and back threads in the order in which they are inserted
- Insert the face weave on face thread only using normal convention for warp backing and reversed convention for weft backing.
- Insert back weave on back threads only based on normal reversed convention as before taking care to place a mark of the back weave between 2 long floats of the face weave thus concealing the binding marks of the back weave by covering float on the face.

- It may be noted that warp faced weaves are more suitable for warp backing and weft faced weave for weft backing and certain square faced weaves can be successfully applied to both.

1. **Weft Backed Cloths**

- More soft cloth obtained in weft backed cloth owing to the weft containing less twist and being under less tension than warp.
- The standard order of arranging the picks in weft-backed cloth are

1. 1 face to 1 back
2. 2 face to 1 back
3. 3 face to 1 back
4. 2 face to 2 back
5. 4 face to 2 back

- Cost of weaving is less for 3 and 5 as these one only half as many backing picks per cm.
- Convention is reversed while marking the design in design paper.

2. Reversible Weft-Backed Weaves

- Same weft face weave formed on both sides.
- The backing weave is shown by crosses placed on the backing picks

- Sateen weaves are more suitable than twill as they form smoother surface.
- By employing differently coloured wefts for the face and back a cloth is produced in which the two sides are differently coloured.

Methods of Weft-Backing Standard Twill and Hopsack Weaves

- In a 2-and-2 twill weft backing can be arranged 1 face 1 back and the weave on the under side may be 1-and-3 twill.
- 8 thread sateen can be used for the back weave and 2-and-2 twill for the face weave, the cloth will be looser and softer in the back.
- 2-and-2 hop sack weave can also be used for face weave in weft backing.
- The proportion 2 face and 1 back or 1 face and 1 back or 2 face and 2 back can be used.
- The back weave can be satin or 8 thread sateen.
- It is better to place the backing pick between two face picks that are in the same shed.
- In case of 2-and-2 hopsack weave backed with 8 thread sateen in the proportion 1 face and 1 back only half the stitches of the back weave can be arranged with face weft floats on both sides.
- In such case the mark should be covered by a covering face pick which will conceal the by subsequent beating up.

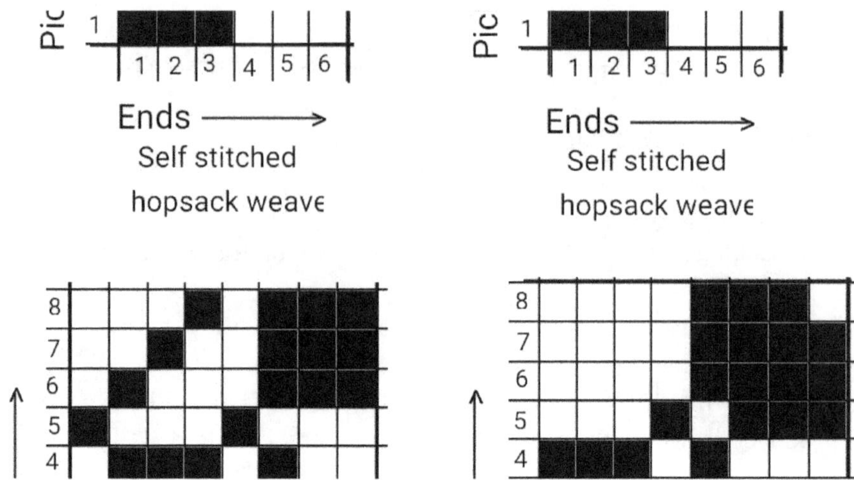

Standard Twill and Hopsack Weaves

Warp-Face Weaves Backed with Weft

- The back weave is looser than the face weave.
- 4 thread warp twill can be used for face and 8-thread sateen for back weave
- 5 thread satin can be used for face and 10-thread sateen for back

Method of Selecting Weft Ties for Irregular Weaves

- The ties for face weaves that are regular in construction are easily arranged, but before constructing a backed design, it is convenient to indicate the face weave lightly and to scheme the distribution or the ties by inserting back weave marks between the sequences.
- The ties for irregular weaves are sometimes difficult to arrange. In such cases a convenient method to arrange is:

- The positions of the backing picks in the order in which they are inserted with face picks are indicated.
- First, ties are marked between the face picks where only one tying position is available.

- Second, the ties are marked on the ends which can afford only one surface tying position.
- Third, ties are marked in remaining position can been taken to indicate one for each backing pick.
- If a tie has already been indicated in an end, another tie should not be indicated in the same end i.e. in each end there should be only one tie.
- If in case there is no option to mark the tie between two face picks due to the presence of the previous tie, it is better to place the stitch with a face weft float on one side only.

1. Warp Backed Cloths

- Arrangement of 2 series of warp to 1 series of weft
- More economical compared with weft backed principle.
- Formation of stripe patterns in the underside is possible which is not possible in weft backed fibre
- More stronger than weft back cloth
- Drawing in the warp is more costlier because there is more number of warp
- Low quality of backing yarn cannot be used.
- Drafts are usually more complicated and greater no: of heals are required in producing similar effects.
- Standard order of arranging ends in warp backed cloths are 1 face to 1 back, 2 face to 1 back, 3 face and 1 back
- In some cases a backed weave is combined in stripe form with a single weave.

Reversible Warp-Backed Weaves

- The 3-and-1 twill on both sides is a standard reversible weave with a difference in a direction twill.
- 4 thread and 5 thread satin weaves can also be made reversible.

Beaming and Drafting Warp-Backed Structures

- In beaming the warp for a warp backed cloth preferably 2 series of warp threads are placed on separate beams.

- In drafting warp-backed design simple pattern may be drawn straight over.
- The backing ends may be intermingled with those upon which the face ends are drawn.
- It is better to draw each series through a separate set of healds. In cases where has is difference in thickness or material between the face and backing ends or if the face weave requires a special draft.

Methods of Warp Backing Standard Weaves

The example of standard methods of placing back weaves ties are

- Twill (1 X 5 or 2 X 4) order of stitching with 3-and-3 twill face weave
- 3 thread twill on both sides with 2 face and 1 back arrangement form twill running in the same direction when the cloth is turned over.
- 2-and-2 hopsack face weave with alternate order of back stitching in 2 face and 1 back order.
- 2-and-2 hopsack face weave backed in 4 sateen order in 2 face and 1 back order.
- In a 2-and-2 hopsack weave in 1 face and 1 back order back weave may form 4 thread twill or satin but in each case one half the stitches are covered by a face float on one side only.

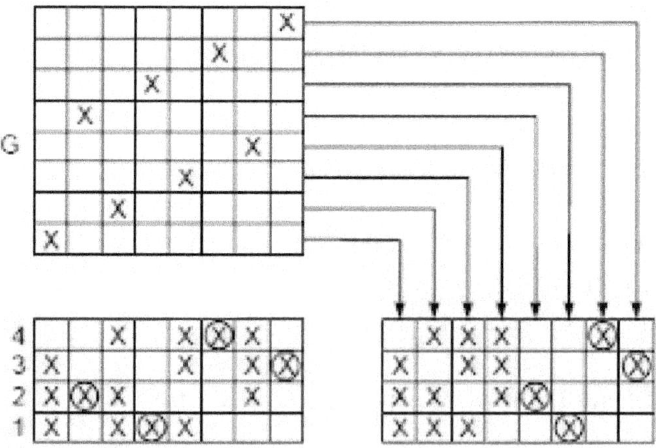

Warp Backing Standard Weaves

Method of Selecting Warp Ties for Irregular Weaves

- The face weave is marked in, and the position of the backing ends-in the order in which they are arranged with the face are indicated below the face plan.
- The ties are first indicated between the face ends in the places where only one tying position is available.
- The remaining ties are indicated in the position which will give the more regular and uniform distribution.

<u>POINTS TO REMEMBER</u>

- Extra threads may be introduced either as weft or warp or in a combination of warp and weft
- For extra warp figuring- a separate warp beam is required for each warp on account of the different take up rates between the extra and the ground ends.
- For extra weft figuring- The weaving machine must have the capacity to insert more than one colour or kind of weft.
- The extra threads may be inserted in continuous order or in intermittent order.

- In the ground of ordinary extra warp figured fabrics, it is necessary to make extra threads to be invisible from the face side.
- Denting plan: The ground ends are dented regularly two per dent with figuring ends being added to some dents as they occur, so that in some splits there may be four ends, in some three and in some others only two ground ends.

- Replacement of one colour of extra weft by another in succeeding horizontal rows of design is known as chintzing

SUGGESTED QUESTIONS:
SECTION A
1.Define Denting plan.
2. Define Chintzing.
3. Define Extra warp figuring.
4. Define Extra weft figuring.

SECTION B

1. Differentiate Extra Warp and Extra Weft Figuring.

2.Write the methods of Disposing of the Surplus Threads.

3.Write short note on warp backed fabric

4.Write short note on weft backed fabrics.

SECTION C

1. Write in detail about extra warp figuring single colour.

2. Discuss extra warp figuring two colours.

3. Write in detail about extra weft figuring single colour.

4. Explain extra weft figuring two colours.

CHAPTER IV

Pile Fabric

AIMS & OBJECTIVES

In this chapter we will discuss about the pile fabric and its formation.this chapter gives extra knowledge about the weft pile – plain back, twill back – length, density and fastness of pile – corduroy weft plush. Warp pile – Terry pile, with the aid of wires, face to face warp pile etc.

Pile fabrics

- Pile fabrics are characterized by the brush like surface formed by tufts of warp or weft cut threads.
- The brush like surface is formed by a set of threads which project at right angles from a foundation or ground structure and form a pile or loop on the surface.
- Cutting the looped threads can be done either on the loom or on the machines of the fabric finishing department.
- Such fabrics should be distinguished from the others which become a pile after passing through a raising machine or after electrical flocking
- In pile fabrics a proportion of the threads, either warp or weft, are made to project at right angles from a foundation texture and form a pile on the surface.
- The projecting threads may be cut or uncut thus resulting in tufted or looped pile.

Classification of pile fabrics

Pile Fabric

Weft Pile Faric/ Velveteen Warp Pile Fabric / Velvet

All over or Pile Terry Piles

Weft Plushes Wire Piles

Corded Velveteens or Fustains Fast Structures Loose Structures

Figured Veleveteens

Weft pile fabrics

- Composed of one series of warp threads and two series of weft threads, the ground and the pile.

- Weft pile structure called velveteen's have very high density may reach upto 200 picks per cm.
- Pile effect is not produced during weaving but is a result of a cutting operation during cloth finishing.
- The surface of the cloth is covered by weft floats that are severed by knife action and form the cut pile surface.
- The ground cloth, usually plain or twill, is unaffected by the knife action and forms a solid base from which the cut tuffs project and in which they are anchored.
- Before cutting the cloth is prepared for the operation by stiffening the surface float to define the cutting races more precisely and to ensure crisper cutting.
- The back of the cloth is treated with an adhesive to ensure that the tuffs during cutting are not plucked out from the ground structure.
- The fabrics after cutting undergo a crosswise brushing operation and are then singed and dyed.
- Weft pile fabrics are classified as

- All over or plain velveteens.

- Weft plushes.
- Corded velveteens
- Figured weft pile fabrics.

All over or plain velveteens

- They have a perfectly uniform surface, with the foundation surface uniformly covered by short pile of equal length.
- Main points to note in constructing designs are

- The weaves that are used for the ground and pile.
- The ratio of pile picks to ground picks.

- These factors together with EPI and PPI of the cloth influence length, density and fastness of pile.
- The ground weaves mostly used are plain, 2-and-1 twill and 2-and-2 twill.

- The pile and ground picks may be arranged in any reasonable proportion, but generally a particular ratio is most suitable for a given weave.

Plain back velveteens

- The foundation weave is plain weave.
- The base weave for pile interlacing may be plain, twill, satinette or 5 thread sateen.
- The number of pile picks to each ground pick is equal to the number of picks in the repeat of the pile base weave.
- Pile base weaves are indicated only on alternate ends; thus each plan is on twice as many ends as the base weave.
- Different pile base weave result in different weft floats

  - Pile weave base with Plain weave :-3 floats- Design is arranged 2 pile picks to one ground picks

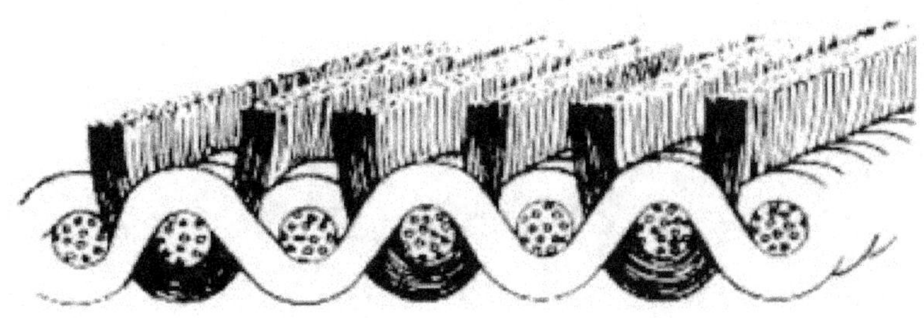

Plain Back

- Pile weave base with 1-and-2 twill :-5 floats- design is arranged in 3 picks to one ground pick.
- Pile weave base with 1-and-3 twill :- 7 floats- design is arranged in 4 picks to one ground pick
- Pile weave base with Satinette weave:-7 floats - design is arranged in 4 picks to one ground pick
- Pile weave base with 5 thread sateen:-9 floats- design is arranged in 5 picks to one ground pick

- All the piles go into the same shed as the first ground pick, but are in the opposite shed to the second ground pick.
- In the fabric the ground picks are entirely concealed by the floating pile picks.
- Each float pile stands out furthest from the foundation cloth at its centre. The centres of the floats occur only on alternate ends.
- The guide of the cutting knife is so adjusted that only those floats are engaged whose centres are in line with longitudinal movement of the knife.
- After the cutting process, the twist runs out of the free ends of the weft threads which thin project vertically from the foundation in the form of tuffs of fibres.

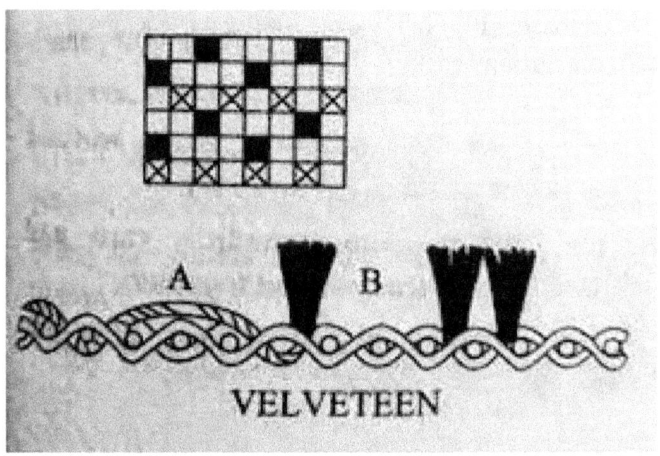

Velveteen

Twill back velveteens.

Velveteen

- Foundation weave is twill which may be 1-and-2 twill or Genoa, 2-and-2 twill etc.
- Twill foundation weave is looser than a plain, so it requires a large number of ground piles to be inserted.
- As a result more pile picks can be inserted for a given ratio of ground and pile picks which forms a denser pile.
- The pile picks can be arranged in the proportion of the 2, 3, or 4 to each ground pick.
- The 2-and-1 twill foundation weave and 1-and-2 twill pile base with a ratio of 2 pile to one ground produces a standard moleskin class of fabric

Twill back Velveteen

- Moleskin fabric is made in coarse cotton yarns. This is not a pick fabric as the floating piles are not cut but remain in the condition they are after weaving.
- The 2-and-2 twill foundation weaves with irregular 6-thread sateen pile base with a ratio of 3 piles to one ground. This is a fast pile structure

CORDUROY WEFT PLUSHES

- These constructions are similar in the principle to the ordinary all over velveteens
- They are made with longer pile floats and in heavier weights being chiefly employed as upholstery cloths.
- The pile weft is anchored to the ground cloth on the fast pile principle.
- The structure with plain foundation, 8-thread irregular sateen weave as pile interlacing in a ground: pile ratio as 2:1 results in a heavy type of weft plush termed as 'dogskin'.

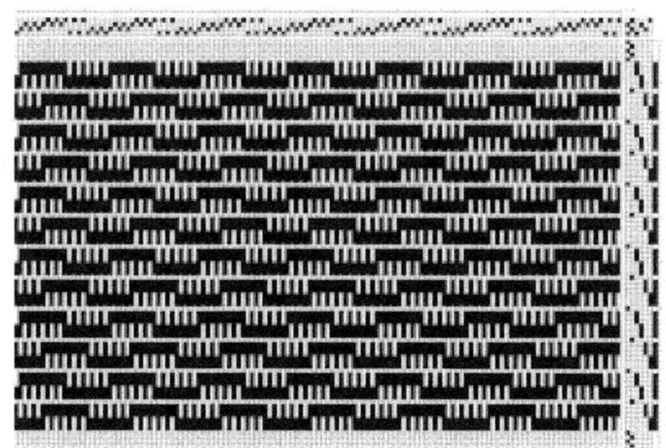

CORDUROY WEFT PLUSHES

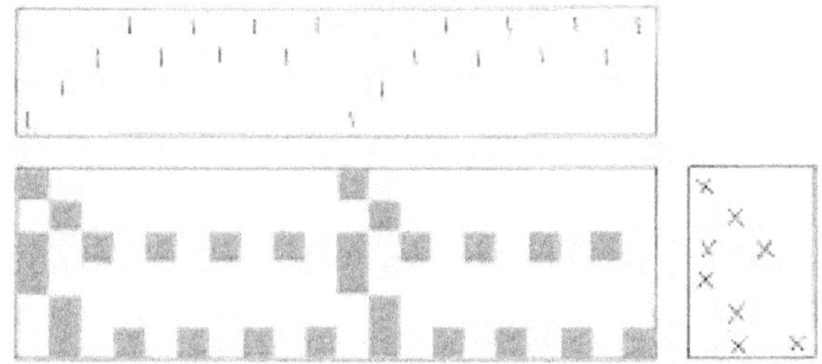

CORDUROY WEFT PLUSHES- Draft

- Variety of effect in the plush can be obtained by having the pile picks alternately in different colours or different materials.
- By arranging the pile picks alternately in different colours or materials, stripes of pile are formed on the surface.
- Reversible weft plush structure is used to luxurious rugs.
- Reversible weft plush cloths have plain ground texture and pile binding places are arranged in 6-sateen order colour from that on the face

Corded velveteens

- In these structures, the pile picks are bound in, at intervals, in a straight line.
- The tuffs of fibres project from the foundation in the form of cords or ribs running lengthwise of the fabric.
- The finer classes of cords are made in fine yarns with a plain back and heavier fabrics like men's clothing are made with a twill ground weave. In the simplest cord designs the pile picks are bound in plain order on two consecutive ends.
- The plain binding weave of the pile picks may be reversed in alternate cords and the design extends over the width of 2 cords and each pile pick forms alternately a long and a short float.
- One side of each tuff is longer than the other side and this difference in length causes the ribs to have a rounded formation.
- The long side of the tuffs forms the centre and the short side the outer parts of the cords.
- 2-and-1 twill, 2-and-2 twill may also be used as back or foundation weave. The ratio of the pile: ground may be 2:1.
- If the sides of the tuffs are of equal length the ribs will not be rounded.

Corded velveteens

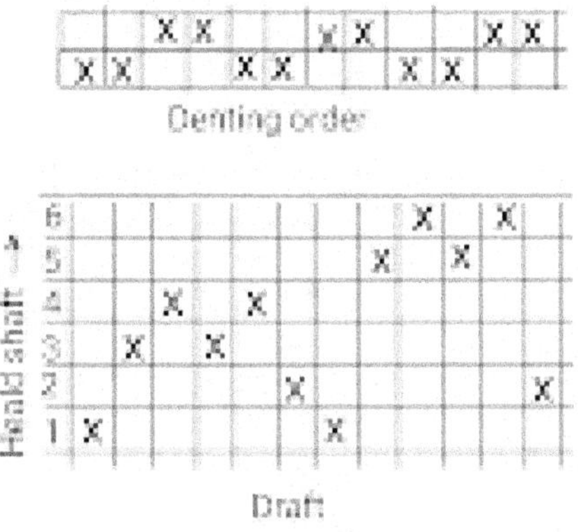

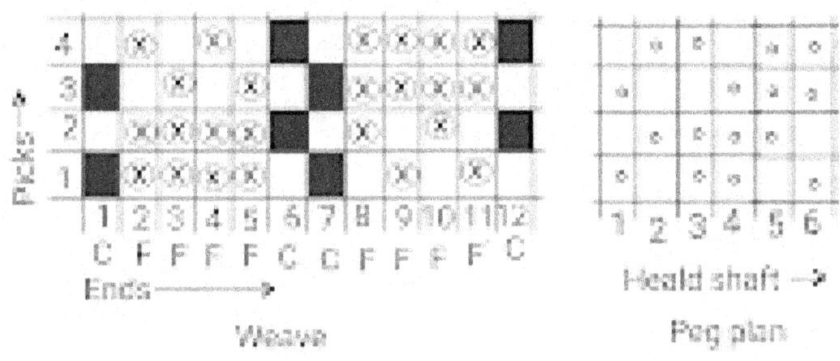

Corded weave

Figured weft pile fabrics

- These structures are not produced at present on account of very high costs of weaving and finishing.

Figured velveteens

- The fabric surface is occupied by a massive pile figure and the bare ground is exposed only to separate the parts of the ornamental part of the design.

- Any velveteen weave can be used in which the pile weft is prevented from showing on the surface.
- There are two methods of disposing of the surplus weft in the ground

a. It is bound in on the under side in the same manner as on the face.
b. It is floated loosely on the back of the foundation texture and after the cutting operation is brushed away as waste.

Figured cords

- Any standard cord weave may be employed as the basis of the structure.
- The styles are limited to simple geometrical figures.
- The ground effect is produced by floating the pile weft on the back between the binding ends.
- In check patterns the horizontal lines can be formed simply by discontinuing the pile weave and inserting the required number of ground picks consecutively.

1. **Length of the pile.**

- Length of piles varies based on

a. Ends per cm of the cloth.
b. No of ends over which the pile weft floats.

  ◦ Increased length of pile obtained by

a. reducing ends per cm

  or

a. Increasing no: of ends over while pile weft floats

  ◦ Decreased length of pile result from

a. increasing ends per cm

  or

b. reducing the pile float.

2. **Density of the pile.**

- Density of the pile varies according to the

a. the thickness of the weft
b. the number of tuffs in the given space.
c. Length of the pile.

- Increase in thickness of the weft makes the pile coarser.
- A long pile causes the surface of the cloth to be better covered and thus gives a filler handle than a short pile
- Greater the length the pile is, the fewer are the number of tuffs formed by each pile pick.

  No: of tuffs per cm² = ends per cm × pile picks per cm
  Ends in repeat of pile weave

3. **Fast pile structures**

- Important features of such fabrics is the proper securing of the pile to the foundation cloth so that there will be no tendency of the tuffs fraying out.

- In normal structures with v-type binding the tuffs are bound in by only one end at a place and so the fastness of the pile is chiefly dependent upon the pressure of the picks one another.

- The structure with fewer picks per cm can be secured by interweaving the pile picks more frequently with w-type binding and making them 'fast pile'.

- The former interweaving renders it more difficult to insert larger amounts of weft.

- In a fast pile structure, the richness of the cloth will suffer but the greater firmness gives the cloth better weaving quality.

Types of binding

- There are two types or binding pile threads.

  (a) V-type:- it is easy to tighten but the draw back is it can be taken out easily
  (b) W-type secures the pile more firmly to the ground fabric.

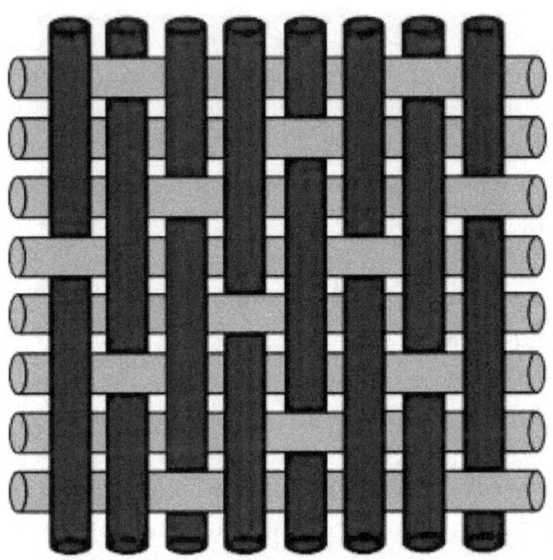

Binding

1. Warp pile fabrics

- These structures consist of piles or loops of warp yarn running lengthwise along the fabrics.

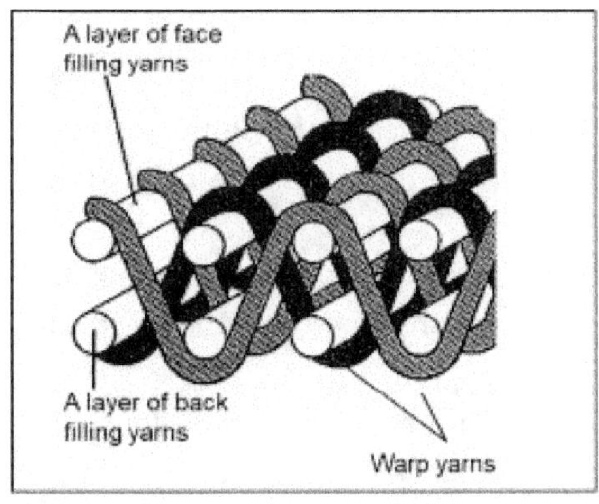

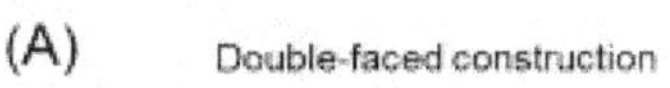

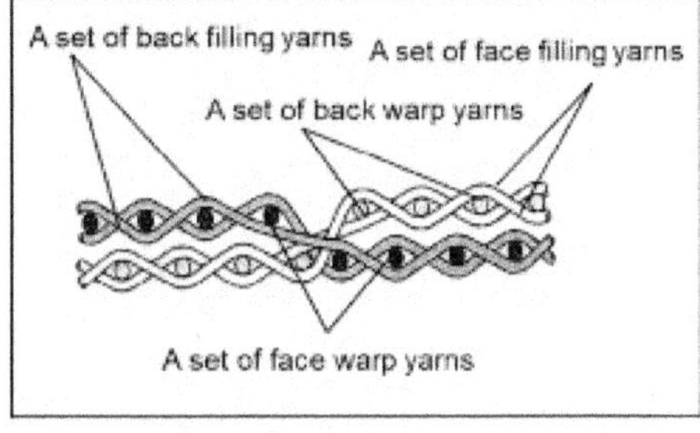

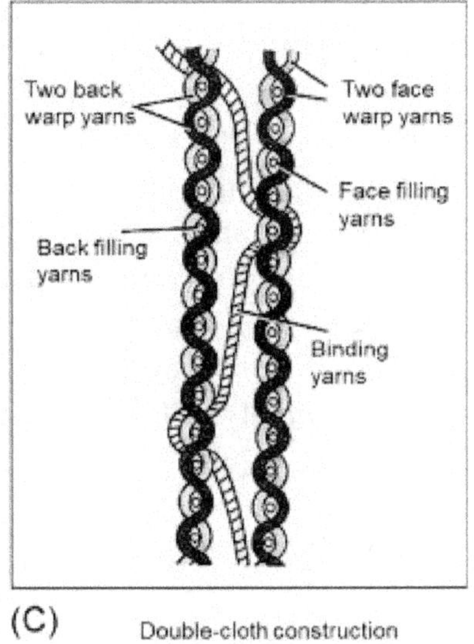

Warp Pile Fabric Structure

- Two systems of warp threads are necessary for weaving warp pile fabrics i.e. pile warp and ground warp and one system of weft.
- The pile warp is supplied from a special weavers beam.
- The length of the pile yarn is considerably greater than that of the ground yarn.
- When the pile fabrics are produced with shortcut dense pile they are known as velvets.
- There are three methods of constructing warp pile structures

a. Terry pile
b. With the aid of wires.
c. Through face to face principle.

Terry pile structures

- Also known as turkish toweling.
- Warp ends are made to form loops on the surface of the cloth.
- Ground warp and weft threads from the ground cloth on which the loops are formed by the pile ends.
- The loop may be formed on one side or both sides.
- One thread may alternate between face and back of the cloth for ornamentation purpose.
- The looped structure is suitable for toweling purposes as the long, free floats of yarn made from absorbent materials are capable or wicking up large amounts of moisture.
- The materials that are used are cotton, linen and viscose rayon staple yarn.

Formation of pile

- The formation of terry pile depends on creation of gap between the fell of cloth and two succeeding picks of weft.

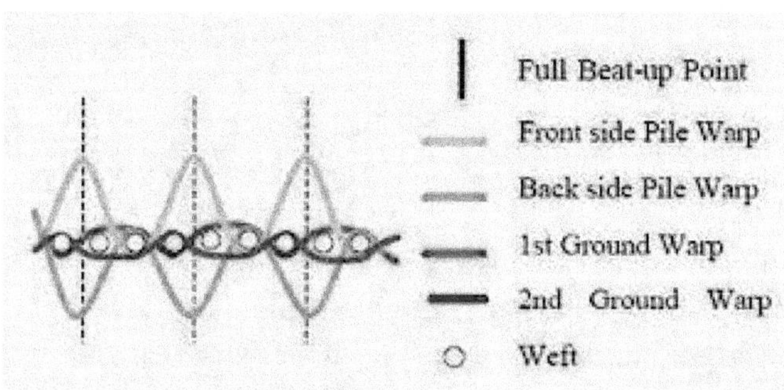

Pile Formation

- The length of gap depends on height of pile required and it forms un-interlaced warp floats.
- To form the gap two succeeding picks are beaten up short of the true cloth fell and produce a temporary false fell.

- On the third pick of the group full beat up takes place and the three piles are together pushed to the true fell position.
- They cannot slide between pile ends because

a. They are structurally locked and
b. The pile warp at that moment is slack.

- They pull a length of pile warp from the beam and force the excess length of pile yarn in front of them into a loop.
- Warp float on face surface form loop on face side and the float on back surface form loop on back side of fabric.
- There are two ways of creating gap between fell of cloth and the weft

a. Reed is drawn back the requirement distance before reaching the

fell of the cloth
b. Fell of the cloth itself is made to recede away from the oncoming reed during the insertion of the two succeeding picks.

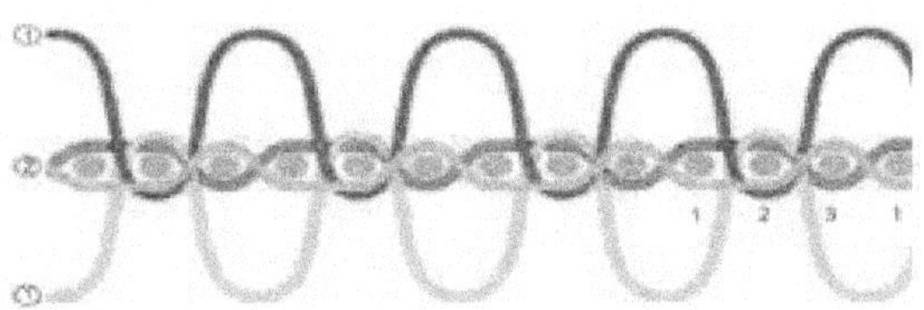

Three pick Terry

Different terry pile structures are given as:-

- 3 picks pile structure.

- In a 3 picks pile structure 3 picks need to be inserted to make one horizontal row of loops- V –type binding is used

- 4 picks pile structures

- In a 4 picks pile structure 4 piles need to be inserted to make one horizontal row of loop

- 5 picks pile structures

- In a 5 picks pile structure 5 piles need to be inserted to make one horizontal row of loop

- 6 picks pile structures

- In a 6 picks pile structure 6 picks need to be inserted to make one horizontal row of loop as opposed to only three in a 3 pick fabrics - W –type binding is used
- To produce the same pile coverage in a 6-pick, as in a 3-pick cloth twice as many picks per cm are required

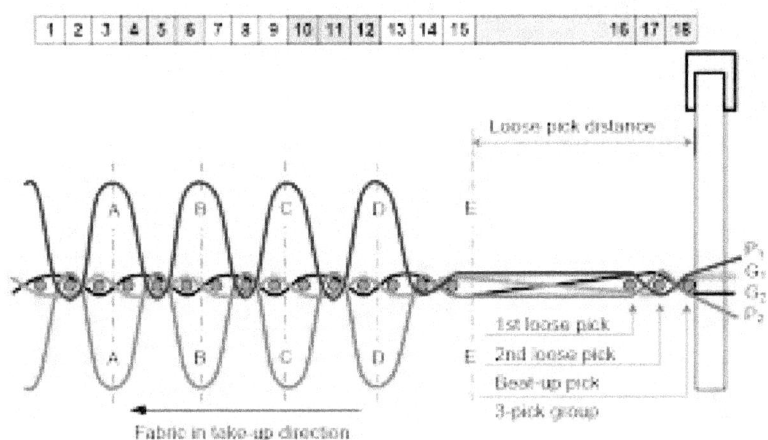

-

Terry Pile weave on both sides

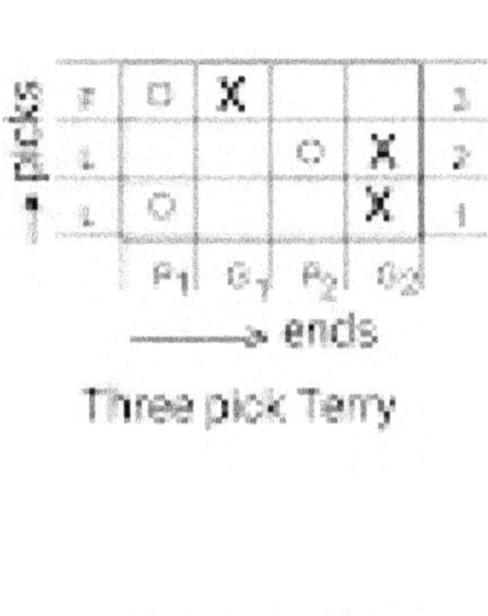

Three pick Terry

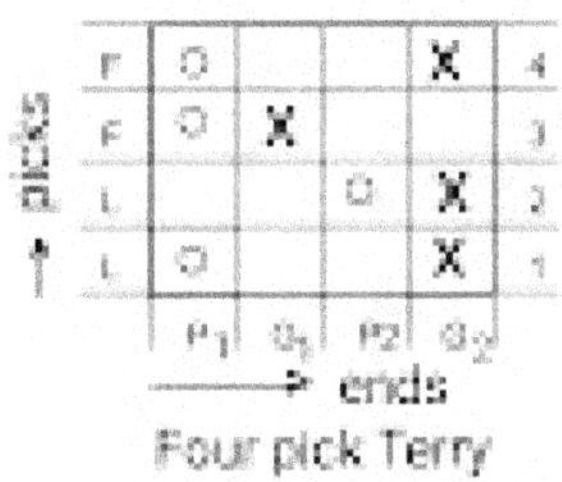

Four pick Terry

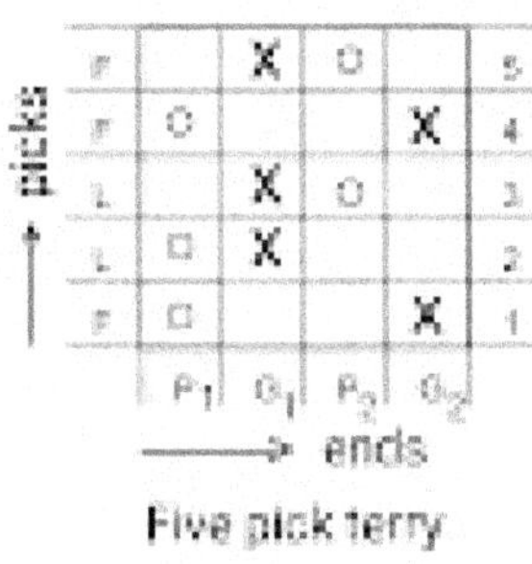

Five pick terry

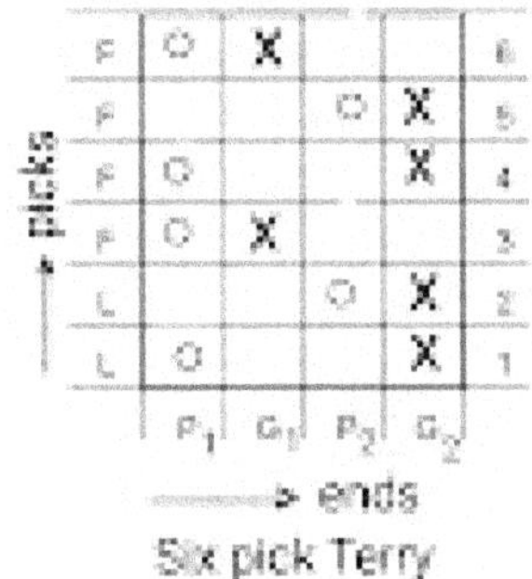

Six pick Terry

○ - Pile end up
× - Ground end up

Terry Pile

Terry ornamentation

- Terry ornamentation consists of introducing colored pile threads to form stripes.
- If the loops are formed on both sides of the cloth one side may be colored independently of the other.
- The pile yarns may be caused to form loops first on one side and then on other side of the cloth which can be used to form simple checks to complex figures
- If the two set of pile yarns are brought from one warp beam all the threads either form pile or lie straight simultaneously on both sides.

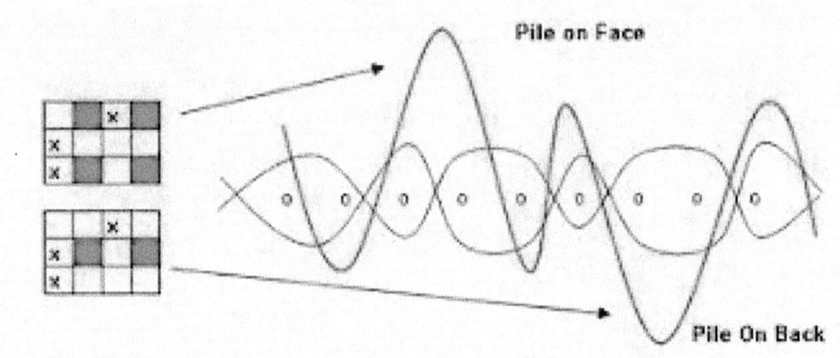

Terry Structure

- If only one series of pile thread is used the loops are formed in the face and back in turn and results ground and pile sections alternately on both sides.
- Different types of terry ornamentation possible are:-
- stripe and check dobby patterns
- figured terry pile fabrics
- Mixed color effects and
- Cut pile terry fabrics.

Green and Red Stripes

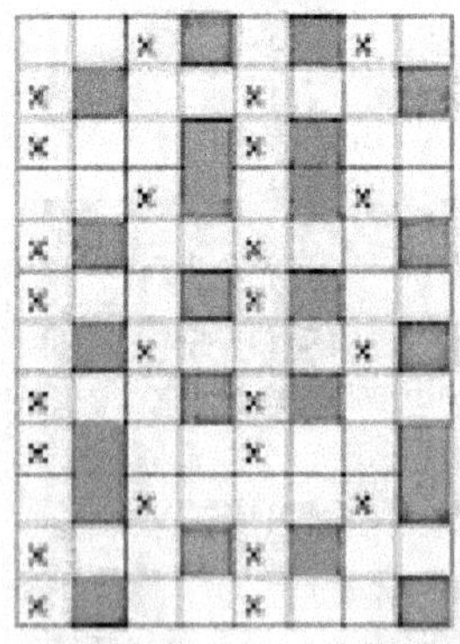

Green and Red Checks

Pile Terry

Warp pile fabrics produced with the aid of wires

- Only one kind of weft and at least two kinds of warp i.e., ground and pile, separately beamed and tensioned is required.
- To produce the pile a wire is inserted across the width of the warp into a shed formed only by the pile ends.

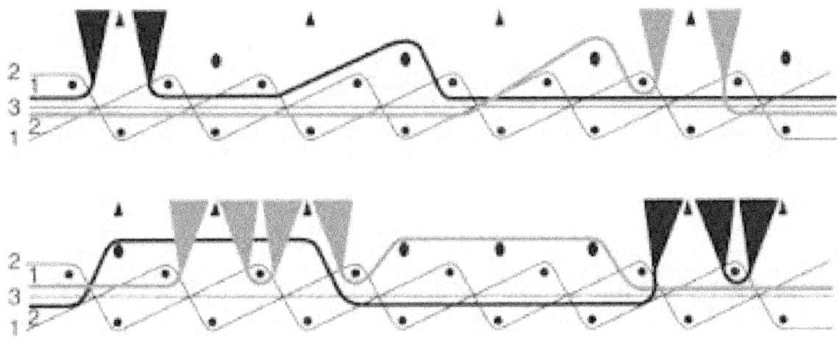

Warp pile fabrics produced with the aid of wires

When the pile ends are subsequently dropped into the bottom shed and interlaced with the weft they remain draped over wires.

- Weft Arrangement- 2G 1Wire

- Warp Arrangement- 2G 1Pile

- Arrangement 6 x 6

- The cross-section dimension of the wire determine the height of the pile
- After the insertion of a no: of weft and wires, the wire farthest from the fell of the cloth is withdrawn and reinserted in the fell to form new wire loops.
- There may be 12-50 wires between the point of withdrawal and insertion.
- The special mechanism inserts the wire rapidly and withdrawn slowly.
- The pile may be looped, if plain wires are used.

The pile may be cut, if the wire has a cutting blade as its tip end

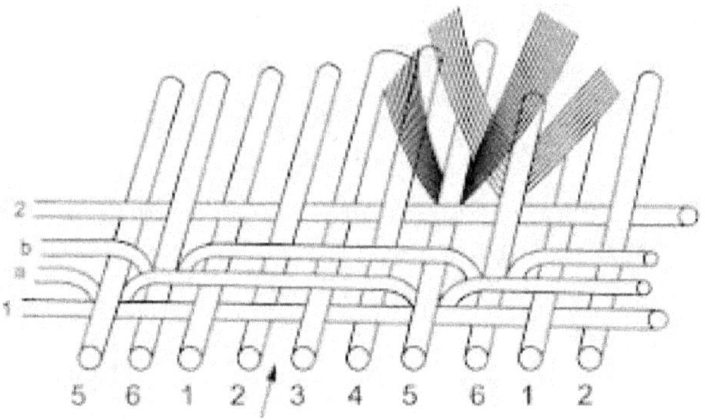

Pile Fabric

- The wires vary in shape according to whether the pile is to be looped or cut.
- Most of the cutting wires are made disposable razor-type cutting edge which put into a slot at the tip.
- The circular cross-section wire is suitable for the production of short pile.
- Long pile is produced on wires with a rectangular cross section.
- The depth of the wires range from 1.5 mm to 2.5 mm
- This mechanism requires at the side of the loom a space which is at least equal to the width of cloth being woven.
- The wire pile fabrics can be grouped in three main classes.
- All over or continuous pile structures
- Figuring with one series of pile threads.
- Figuring with several series of pile threads.

Warp pile fabrics produced on the face to face principle.

- These types of warp pile fabric contains
- Three systems of warp: - face end, back end and pile end.
- Two systems of weft: - face pick and back pick.
- Where face weave and back weave are called ground weave.
- The face and back fabrics are stitched on the loom by means of pile warp.

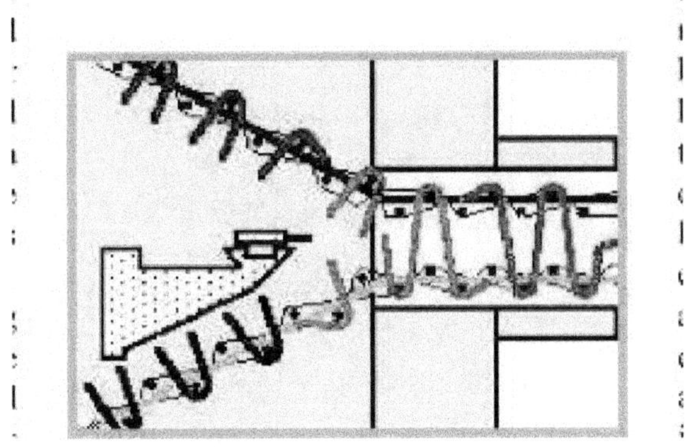

Face to Face pile

- The two fabrics are separated by cutting the pile threads.
- A separate weavers been is necessary in weaving warp pile.
- The representative fabric is velvet.

Method of weaving

- Two ground cloths are produced with a certain space between them.
- The distance from face to back fabrics determines the required height of the pile.
- Pile end interface alternately with face and back picks.
- According to the shedding and picking during the weaving the method of weaving is classified as

a. Single shedding in which face cloth is formed by face ends and picks and back cloth is formed by back ends and picks.
b. Double shedding in which face and back cloths are formed simultaneously, identically interlacing ends are drawn into two mail heads. Here face and picks are inserted in pairs

Cutting

- The two fabrics are separated by cutting the pile threads in the middle during the weaving process.

- Cutting is done when the race is put back and the pile ends are taut.
- Each cloth is wound separately

Development of the weave for pile constructed face to face principle

- Selection of weave. Normally for velvet 1/1 pain, 2/2 weft rib and 2/1 varied rib are selected.
- The density of pile and the distribution of the pile need to be considered while selection.
- Determine the ways of binding type, v-type is preferable compared with w-type.
- Determine the ratio of the ground and the pile warp
- For e.g.: - the parameters are.

- V-type binding
- Warp: 1 pile end-1 face-1 back-1 pile end-1 face-1 back end
- Weft: 1 face-1 back pick
- Ground: plain weave for face and back weaves

  - The weave is constructed by following steps

    - Determine the repeats and draw outline
    - Draw the longitudinal section

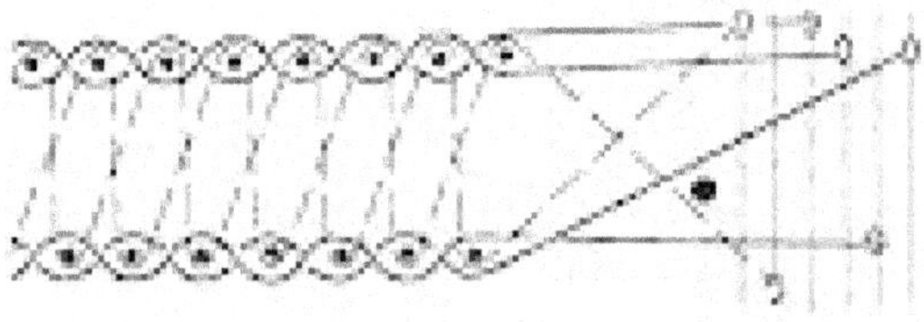

Fig. 8.6

- ○

Pile

  - Transfer the weave.

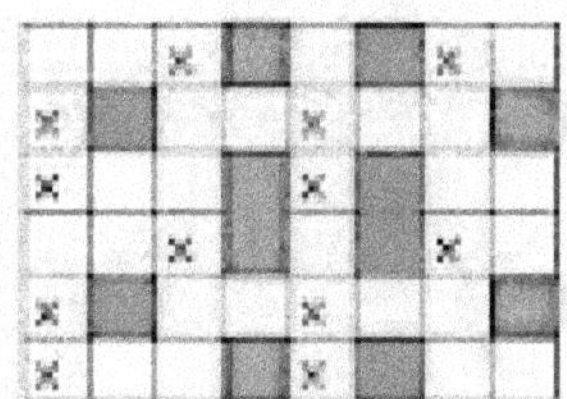

Structure

POINTS TO REMEMBER

- Pile fabrics are characterized by the brush like surface formed by tufts of warp or weft cut threads.
- Weft pile structure called velveteen's have very high density may reach upto 200 picks per cm.
- No: of tuffs per cm² = <u>Ends per cm × pile picks per cm</u>

  Ends in repeat of pile weave

- There are two types or binding pile threads.
- V-type:- it is easy to tighten but the draw back is it can be taken out easily
- W-type secures the pile more firmly to the ground fabric.
- Terry pile structures are also known as turkish toweling.

SUGGESTED QUESTIONS:

SECTION A

1.EPI means _________
2. Name the two types of binding pile threads.
3. Terry pile structures are also known as _______ toweling.
4. Weft pile structure called as ___________.

SECTION B

1.Explain corduroy.
2.Explain weft plush.
3.Explain Warp pile fabrics.

4.Write notes on Terry pile,

5.Give the classification of Pile fabric.

SECTION C

1.Explain the formation of pile.

2.Explain plain back weft pile.

3.Explain twill back weft pile.

4.Write notes on length, density and fastness of pile.

5.Describe briefly face to face warp pile.

6.Explain Warp pile fabrics produced with the aid of wires.

CHAPTER V

Double Clothing

AIMS & OBJECTIVES

In this chapter we will discuss about the formation of Double cloth. This chapter gives extra knowledge about the self stitched – faces to back, back to face, both. Centre stitched – warp and weft and Interchanging double cloth.

1. Double Cloth

Definition

- Double fabric consists of two layers which are woven one above the other.

- This fabric contains two systems of warps, and two systems of weft.

- This fabric can also be called two-ply fabric.
- The upper layer is formed by interlacing the face warp threads with the face weft threads, and the lower layer by interlacing the back warp threads with the back weft threads.

Classification of Double Cloth

Double cloths constructed on the principle of self stitching

- These fabrics contain only two series of threads in both warp and weft directions.
- Stitching of face cloth layer to the back layer is accomplished by occasionally dropping a face end under a back pick or by lifting a back pick over a face pick or by utilizing both the systems

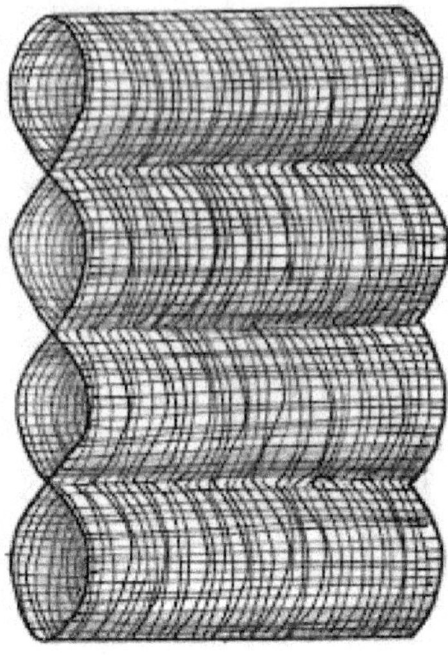

Double cloth structure

Double cloths constructed on the principle of centre thread stitching

- Third series of thread is introduced either in the warp or in the weft direction whose entire function is to stitch the two layers of cloth together.

Double cloths constructed on the principle of stitching by thread interchange

- The stitching of the face and the back cloth is achieved by frequent and continuous interchange of same thread elements between the two cloth layers
- The points at which the threads interchange represents the stitch point.

Double cloths constructed on the principle of cloth interchange

- Complete cloth layers are made to change places in this type.

Stitching between the two fabrics occurs only at the point of cloth interchange.

Double cloths constructed alternately as single and double ply cloths.

- The constituent thread components are occasionally merged together into a heavily set single cloth and occasionally are separated into distinct layers.

Wadded double cloths

- It consists of a face and a back fabric, tied together by floating back ends on face picks or face ends under back picks as in self-stitched double cloths, with the addition of a special series of weft or warp threads introduced independently of the face and back yarns.
- The weft-wadded cloths consist of three series of weft and two series of warp threads.
- The warp-wadded cloths consist of three series of warp and two series of weft threads.
- The wadding threads lie between the two fabrics and are visible neither on the face nor back.

Self-Stitched Double Cloths

- It is composed of two series of warp threads and two series of weft threads; one series of each kind forming an upper or face fabric and the other, an under or back fabric.
- Face picks are arranged in definite order with the back picks and the face ends with the back ends.

- Separate weaves are required for the two fabrics, either alike or different
- Face picks interweave with face ends and back picks interweave with back ends forming two distinct fabrics one above the other.
- The threads of one fabric interweave with the threads of other fabric resulting in the formation of two layers of fabric closely united so that separation of the two layers is impossible.

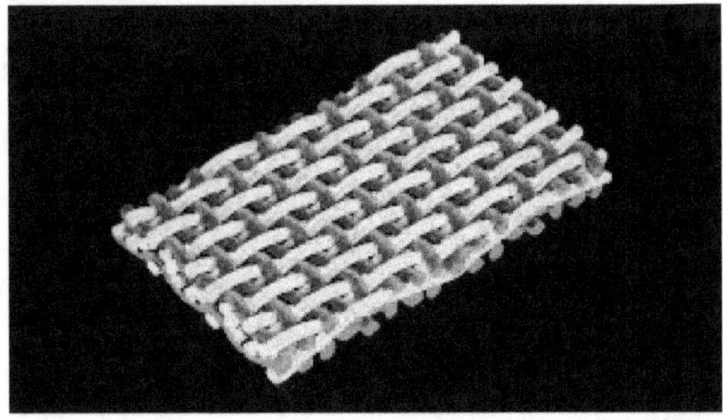

Double Clothing

Selection of the Face and Back Weaves

- The back weave and face weave may be same or contain same relative number of intersections if the threads are arranged in equal proportions.
- For eg. 2- and -2 twill is suitable for backing the 3-up, 2-down, 1-up, 2-down will.
- In the one face and two back arrangements, the plain weave is suitable for backing the 2- and -2 twill and the 2-and -2 hopsack.

Tying or Stitching

- Here stitching is done by either dropping a face end under a back pick or by lifting a back end over a face pick or both.
- A stitch can be made invisible on both sides of the double cloth if

- When the back end is to be raised over the face pick, the back end is used for tying only when it is away from the under side of the back cloth.
- The face pick over which the stitch is made must be away from the face of the top cloth

Face to Back

- If weft sateen or a weft-faced twill weave is used for the face weave, the face ends are dropped down to interlace back weft.

Back to Face

- If warp satin or warp faced twill is employed for the fabric, lifting the back warp over face weft is possible

Double stitching (warp & weft stitching)

- The object of double stitching is to obtain increased firmness of structure

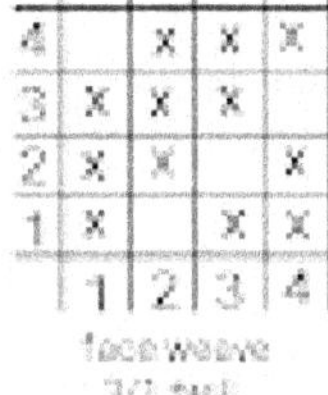

face weave interlacing marks filling

back weave marks interlacing filling

Double cloth

Construction of Squared Paper Designs
Back to face

- The face weave, the back weave and the ties are placed in such positions relative to one another so that the ties are covered on each side of the cloth by the adjacent floats.
- Normal convention in which a mark equals warp is used in the illustrations.
- Face weave and back weave are shown below
- Then insert back weaves on back ends and back picks only.
- Then the stitch marks are introduced by observing the rules for stitch point selection
- The back end is raised to make a stitch when it is absent from the underside i.e. the visible side of the back cloth
- It stitches over the face weft when that weft is absent from the surface of the face cloth.
- When it emerges near the surface of the face cloth it is covered by two adjacent long floats of the face warp.

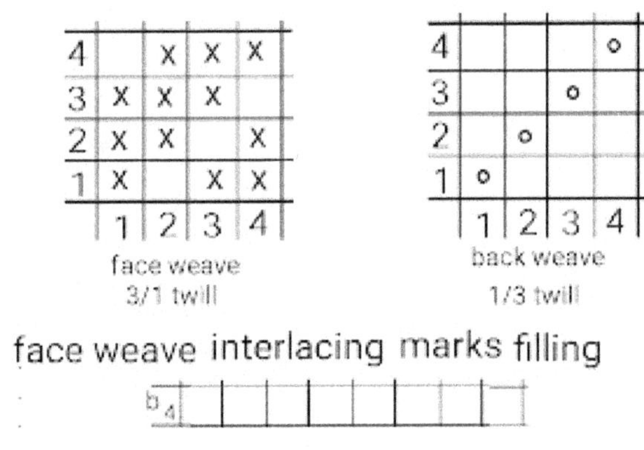

Back to face

Face to back

- The face weave, the back weave and the ties are placed in such positions relative to one another so that the ties are covered on each side of the cloth by the adjacent floats.

- Normal convention in which a mark equals warp is used in the illustrations.
- Face weave and back weave are shown below

Layer separation marks filling

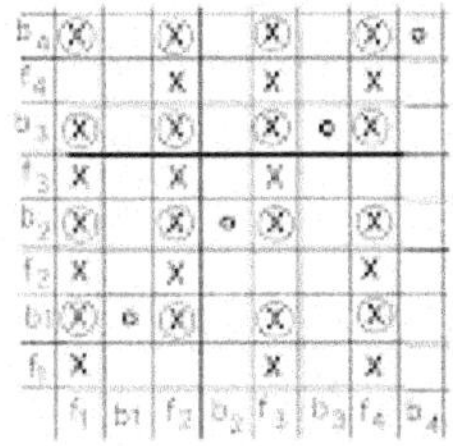

Stitching marks insertion

Raising back end on face pick

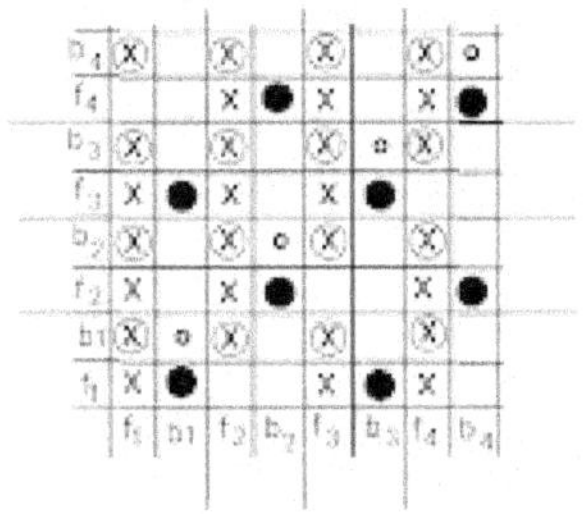

Face to back

- An area equal to one repeat of double cloth is marked.
- Back ends ands picks are indicated in margins with an arrow
- Insert face weaves on face ends and face picks only
- Then insert back weaves on back ends and back picks only

Then the stitch marks are introduced by observing the rules for stitch point selection

- The face end is lowered to make a stitch when it is absent from the upper side i.e. the visible side of the face cloth
- It stitches over the back weft when that weft is absent from the surface of the back cloth.

- When it emerges near the surface of the back cloth it is covered by two adjacent long floats of the back warp.

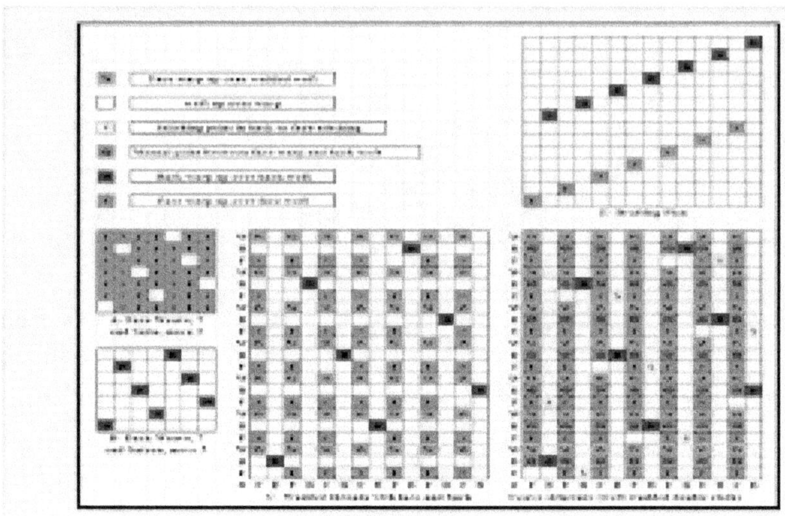

Double clothing weave

Reversible Double Weaves

- By the correct placing of the back weave in relation to the ties same effect can be produced on both sides resulting in a reversible double weaves.

Beaming and Drafting of Self-Stitched Double Cloths

- Two separate warp beams are employed in the construction of double cloths
- Two warps should be held at about same tension.
- The threads in each fabric which work alike may be drawn on the same heald.
- Minimum number of healds in each set is decided by the number of threads in each fabric, which work different from each other.

- The number of healds required in a self-stitched double cloth depends not only on the respective sizes of repeats in the face and the back cloths but also the order of stitching.

Selection of Suitable Stitching Positions

- When the back ends are raised the following conditions should coincide:

- The back end must be at that point away from the underside of the back cloth
- It must 'surface' between two long warp floats of the face weave
- The face pick over which the back end is raised must be absent from the surface of the face cloth
- It must be only pulled down at a point at which its penetration into the back cloth level is covered by two adjacent weft floats on the underside of the back fabric.

- When the face ends are lowered for stitching under the back picks

  - The face end at that point must be absent from the surface of the face cloth
  - It must be lowered at a point at which two long back warp floats cover it on the underside of the back cloth.
  - The back pick at the tie point must be away from the underside of the back cloth
  - It must penetrate towards the surface at a point at which it will be covered by two adjacent face weft floats on the surface of the face cloth.

1. **Centre Stitched Double Cloths**

- A centre thread is introduced with the specific purpose to bind the two fabrics together.
- The threads of one fabric do not interweave with the threads of the other fabric.

- The centre threads oscillate between one and the other and lie between them when not employed for tying.

Centre Warp Stitching

- Face and back cloths are stitched with a centre warp.
- If the colours or counts of the yarns for the face and back differ greatly fine center threads can be used for stitching.
- In centre warp stitching following procedures should be followed

Steps in constructing the point paper Centre Warp Stitching

- In the given example the face and back weave is 2- and -2 twill and the proportion of ends are 1 face and 1 back to 1 centre warp.

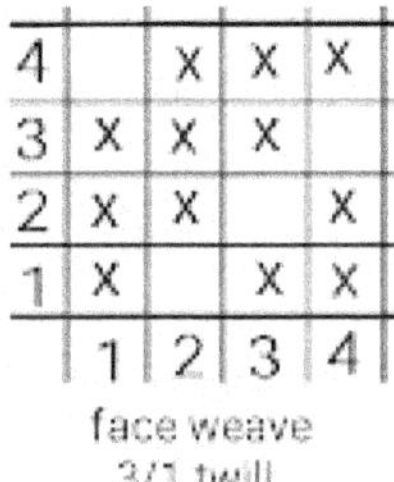

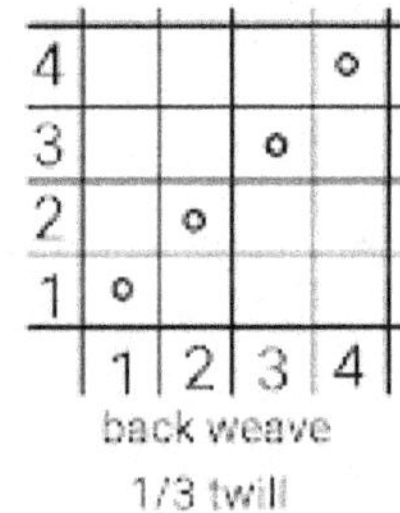

Face and Back weave

- Mark back weave on back ends and back picks.
- Mark face weave on face ends and face picks.
- Where no ties occur the centre warp lies between the face and the back fabric and, therefore, must be lowered on the face picks and raised on the back picks. These are indicated in the design by dots.
- In tying to the face cloth the centre ends are raised over the face picks where these are absent from the face ie., where they are covered by two adjacent floats of the face warp. These are indicated in the design by circles.

- In tying to the back cloths the centre ends are lowered on the back picks where these are absent from the underside i.e., where they are on the underside of the back cloth by two adjacent floats of the back warp. These tying positions are represented by crosses in the designs.

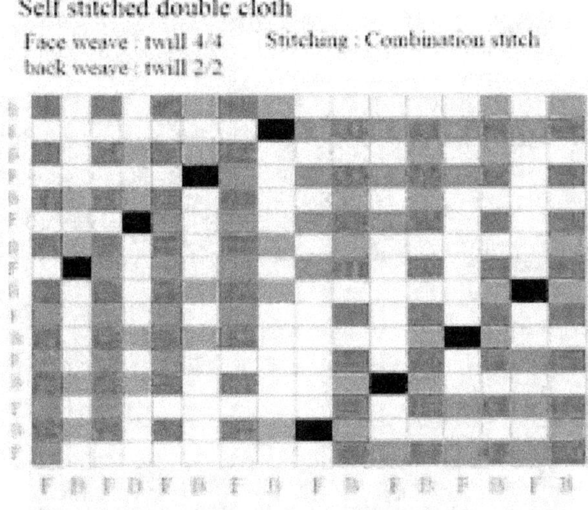

Face and Back pattern

Centre Weft Stitching

- This form of stitching is not very often used since it reduces the rate of cloth production.
- When the centre weft picks are introduced the take-up must be rendered inoperative and thus the picks do not contribute to the length of cloth being produced.
- An example for centre weft is given below.

Steps in constructing the point paper Centre Weft Stitching

- If face and back weave is 2- and -2 twill and the proportion of ends are 1 face and 1 back to 1 centre weft.

- Insert Face weave on face ends and face picks and back weave on back ends and back picks.
- Where no ties occur the centre weft lies between the face and the back cloth. To achieve this face warps are raised and the back ends are lowered on the centre weft. This is indicated by dots in design.
- To achieve a face fabric stitch, a face end must be dropped on a centre pick at a point at which it is absent from the surface i.e., when it is covered by two adjacent floats of the weft. This is indicated by crosses.
- To achieve a back fabric stitch, a back end is raised on a centre pick at a point at which it is absent from the underside of the cloth i.e., when it is covered by two adjacent floats of the back weft. This is indicated by circles.

1. Interchanging Double Cloth

- The two layers of fabric exchange with each other to form the character of the design. It is on these points of interchange that the two cloths are bound together

1. Thread Interchanging

- The interchanging of threads means that the series which actually alternates between the face and back of the cloth can no longer be designated as the face or back yarns because it will occasionally be the one and occasionally be the other.
- The wefts are in the top or the bottom layers across the warp

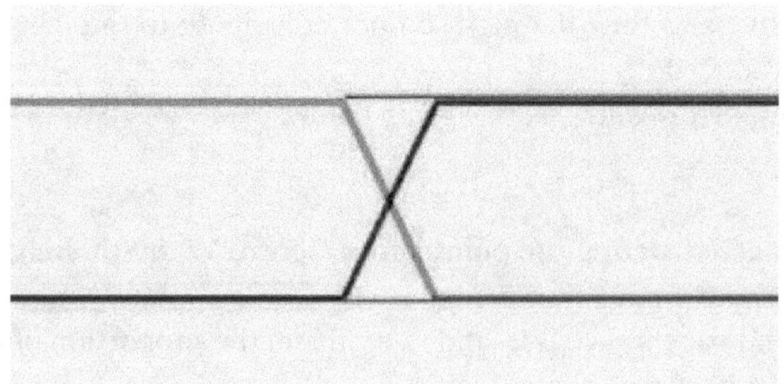

Thread interchanging

- The wefts move between the top and bottom layers across the warp

1. Cloth Interchanging

- Double Cloths can be joined together by interchanging fabric layers.
- The wefts move between the top and bottom layers across the warp.
- In the simple design ranges the effects can be achieved by:

  ◦ Retaining and constant and 1- and -1 colour arrangement in the warp and in the weft while changing the position of separating lifts
  ◦ Retaining the same weave and changing the colour pattern

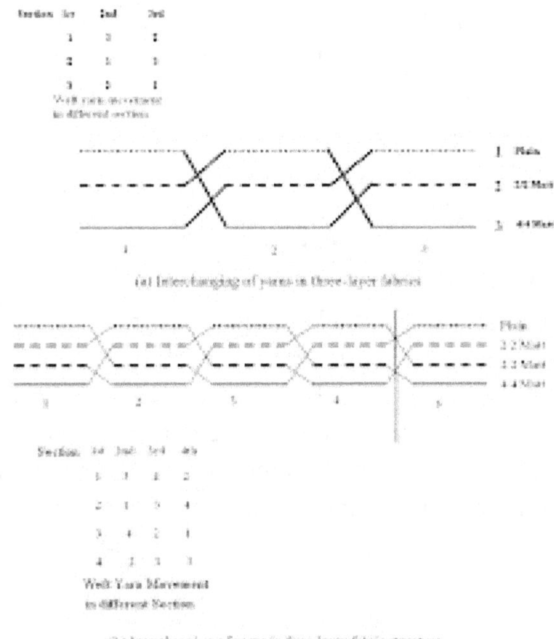

Cloth interchanging

POINTS TO REMEMBER

- Double fabric consists of two layers which are woven one above the other.
- Double fabric contains two systems of warps, and two systems of weft.
- Double fabric can also be called two-ply fabric.
- **Interchanging Double Cloth** - The two layers of fabric exchange with each other to form the character of the design
- Double Cloths can be joined together by interchanging fabric layers.
- The interchanging of threads means that the series which actually alternates between the face and back of the cloth can no longer be designated as the face or back yarns
- **Wadded double cloths** - It consists of a face and a back fabric, tied together by floating back ends on face picks or face ends under back picks as in self-stitched double cloths, with the addition of a special series of weft or warp threads introduced independently of the face and back yarns.

SUGGESTED QUESTIONS:

SECTION A

1.Double fabric can also be called __________.
2. Define double cloth.
3. Define interchanging double cloth.
4. Define wadded double cloth.

SECTION B

1. Give the classification of double cloth.
2. Explain face to back self stitched double cloth.
3. Explain back to face self stitched double cloth.

SECTION C

1. Explain Warp Centre stitched double cloth
2. Explain Weft Centre stitched double cloth
3. Explain interchanging double cloth.